THE HOLY LAND
FOLLOW
THE STEPS
OF JESUS

Etty Boochny

With an Introductory Essay on the Life of Jesus by **Rev. David B. Capes, Ph.D.**
Associate Professor of Christianity, Houston Baptist University

Endorsement by:

Sister Macrina Scott, O.S.F.
Director, Catholic Biblical School of the Archdiocese of Denver

Dr. Jim Fleming, Ed.D.
Executive Director, Biblical Resources Center in Jerusalem, Israel

STEIMATZKY

STEIMATZKY LTD.

Steimatzky House
11, Hakishon Street
P.O.Box 1444
Bnei Brak 51114
Tel. (03) 5775760

Editor and Writer
Etty Boochny

Editorial Advisor & Contributing Writer
Rev. David B. Capes, Ph.D.

Text Consultants
Prof. Joshua Schwartz, Director
Ingeborg Rennert Center for Jerusalem
Studies of Bar-Ilan University, Israel
Yigal Levin
Researches Biblical history and geography,
Land of Israel, Bar-Ilan University, Israel

English Consultants
Louis Markos, Ph.D.
Issy & Paula Miodownik

Art Director
Hanan Yadin

Contributing Designers
Jerry Svajda
Doris Clark
Angela Watson

Production
Jerry Svajda

Lead Photographers
Ami Wallach
Yuri Costa

Contributing Photographers
Hanan Isachar
Chanan Getraide
Garo Photo Studio
Yoel Amster Ltd.
Rick Kelly
Aliza Rahimi
Albatross Aerial Photography
Dolphin Riff Photo by Jeff Rotman
Bible Lands Museum Photos by Z.Redovan
Model of Jerusalem, Second Temple Period,
contributed by Holyland Hotel
Park Timna, contributed by Park Timna

Pre-Press Production
Sharp Imaging Incorporated
N.M.I Enterprises Inc.

The Scripture quotations contained herein are
from the New Revised Standard Version Bible,
copyright 1989 by the Division of Christian
Education of the National Council of Churches
of Christ in the U. S. A., and are used by permission. All rights reserved.

Much thanks to the Mendelbaum and
Boochny families for their great help.

Etty Boochny
Professional tour guide in the Holy Land and
a licensed international tour manager. She
holds a B.A. degree from Bar-Ilan University,
Israel in Land of Israel Studies and Life
Science. Etty started her career as a guide in
Mt. Gillo Field School in the area of
Bethlehem and Jerusalem; since then she has
become a successful tour guide all over the
Holy Land for over ten years. She has written
and edited tour publications about the Holy
Land. Currently, Etty is enrolled in a Master of
Arts program in Theological Studies.

David B. Capes
Associate Professor in the College of
Humanities at Houston Baptist University. He
has degrees from Mercer University (B.A.) and
Southwestern Baptist Theological Seminary
(M.Div. and Ph.D.). Dr. Capes is an ordained
Baptist minister who has served churches in
Georgia, Tennessee and Texas. He has published
books and articles in early Christian theology
and is a popular speaker and guest lecturer.

Although the authors and publisher have
tried to make the information as accurate as
possible, they accept no responsibility for any
loss, injury or inconvenience sustained by any
person using this book.

Distribution world rights by Steimatzky Ltd,
P.O. Box 1444, Bnei Brak 51114, Israel.
Distribution rights in USA and Mexico by
Dror International An N.M.I.Company.

ISBN   0-9662775-1-1

CONTENTS

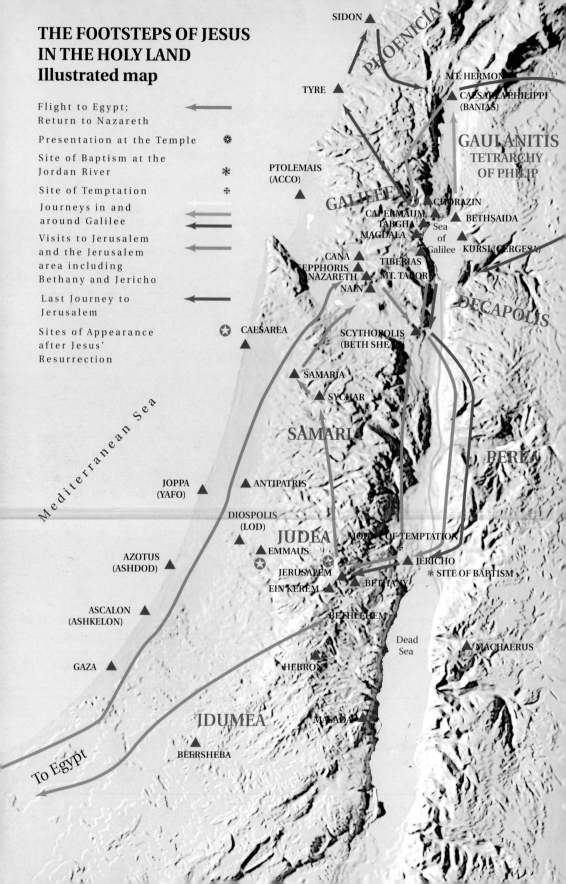

THE FOOTSTEPS OF JESUS IN THE HOLY LAND
Illustrated map

Flight to Egypt;
Return to Nazareth

Presentation at the Temple

Site of Baptism at the
Jordan River

Site of Temptation

Journeys in and
around Galilee

Visits to Jerusalem
and the Jerusalem
area including
Bethany and Jericho

Last Journey to
Jerusalem

Sites of Appearance
after Jesus'
Resurrection

Mediterranean Sea

SIDON

PHOENICIA

TYRE

MT. HERMON

CAESAREA PHILIPPI
(BANIAS)

GAULANITIS
TETRARCHY
OF PHILIP

PTOLEMAIS
(ACCO)

GALILEE

CHORAZIN

CAPERNAUM
TABGHA
MAGDALA

BETHSAIDA

Sea
of
Galilee

KURSI (GERGESA)

CANA
SEPPHORIS
NAZARETH

TIBERIAS
MT. TABOR

NAIN

DECAPOLIS

CAESAREA

SCYTHOPOLIS
(BETH SHEAN)

SAMARIA

SYCHAR

SAMARIA

PEREA

JOPPA
(YAFO)

ANTIPATRIS

DIOSPOLIS
(LOD)

JUDEA

MOUNT OF TEMPTATION

EMMAUS

AZOTUS
(ASHDOD)

JERUSALEM

EIN KEREM

BETHANY

JERICHO

SITE OF BAPTISM

ASCALON
(ASHKELON)

BETHLEHEM

Dead
Sea

MACHAERUS

GAZA

IDUMEA

MASADA

HEBRON

BEERSHEBA

To Egypt

INTRODUCTION

The Holy Land is a unique and beautiful land, rich with a variety of historical, archaeological, and religious sites. Visitors are charmed by its sweeping vistas, hospitable citizens and inspirational images. This country is an enchanting mixture of ancient and modern.

The biblical history that little land reveals lies buried beneath the millennia of settlers and citizens who have called it home. In many places you can simply open the Bible and read about the sights you see. In the Holy Land you can experience the special thrill of walking in the footsteps of Bible characters. Abraham roamed these hills four thousand years ago. About three thousand years have gone by since King David reigned here. But for Christians, **Follow the steps of Jesus in the Holy Land** constitute its ultimate moment. In these regions Jesus, the Son of God, was born. Here he grew in wisdom and stature. Here he was crucified. Here God raised him from the dead.

In this book we take you to the places Jesus knew and loved as recorded in the New Testament Gospels. The book is divided geographically into three regions: north, center and south. In the northern and central regions we describe first those sites Jesus visited and include some of the relevant biblical material. Then we discuss sites which visitors likely see but do not necessarily relate directly to Jesus' ministry. Jerusalem, the sacred city and soul of the country, is given its own section in the chapter on the central region. Although there is no record of Jesus traveling to the southern areas, we have included them because they are significant to the patriarchs, prophets and kings of Judah.

Some who read this book may actually visit the Holy Land and walk in the footsteps of Jesus. Others may simply experience the land of promise in the beautiful pictures, descriptions and scriptures that are included. However you receive and experience this book, we hope that it will unlock for you the message of the Bible and engage your mind and heart in the wonderful world in which Jesus lived.

THE LIFE OF JESUS

No one has had a greater impact upon the world than Jesus of Nazareth. Although He was born to a peasant family, throughout history billions of people have referred to Him as King of Kings and Lord of Lords. He came into the world at a crucial time and place. Scholars tell us He was born between 6 and 4 B.C., a time after the Romans had incorporated the Holy Land into their empire. More than thirty years later He was crucified outside Jerusalem on a Roman cross (ca. A.D. 30).

According to Luke, an angel appeared to Mary in Nazareth and announced that God had chosen her to be the mother of the Messiah. Already Elizabeth, one of Mary's relatives, had conceived a son who would be His forerunner. Elizabeth and her husband were to name him "John." When Mary traveled to Judea to see Elizabeth, John leaped in the womb and the women celebrated God's marvelous plan.

In the final days of pregnancy, Joseph and Mary traveled to Bethlehem to register according to a decree from the Emperor Augustus. While they were there, Mary gave birth to a son and laid Him in a feeding trough for animals. As directed, they named him "Jesus" because he would save his people from their sins. Later, shepherds arrived to see the holy family, telling a story of angelic visits in the night. Some time after, wise men from the east arrived in Bethlehem to pay homage to the child. They had seen a star, a sign that the Messiah of the Jews had been born. King Herod, concerned to maintain his power, began seeking to kill Him. Having been warned about Herod's intentions by a dream, Joseph took Mary and Jesus to Egypt until Herod died a short time later.

The family returned to the Holy Land and settled in their hometown, Nazareth, in the middle of Galilee. When Jesus was twelve years old, His family traveled to Jerusalem to celebrate the feast of Passover. There He amazed the Jewish teachers and His parents with His wisdom and zeal for the things of God.

When Jesus was about thirty years old, He traveled south to the Jordan River to see John the Baptist. He was baptizing in the river all who came and repented of their sins. He proclaimed that God's Kingdom was near. He preached that another more important messenger would come; the stronger would baptize the faithful in the Holy Spirit. Jesus heard John preach and asked to be baptized by him. Although John initially objected, he nevertheless carried through with Jesus' request. After His baptism, God confirmed that He was indeed the Son of God. Immediately Jesus went into the desert to fast, meditate and, according to the Gospels, to be tempted by Satan. These events propelled Jesus into public, itinerant ministry. He left behind the routine of the carpenter shop to engage the world with His prophetic voice.

The Gospels indicate that Jesus began His public ministry in Galilee although some ministry in Judea and Samaria early on cannot be ruled out. He traveled throughout Galilee preaching that the Kingdom of God was at hand and that the people must repent. On the shores of the Sea of Galilee He called fishermen to be His first disciples. In all He chose twelve men to be His closest followers. These would constitute a new people of God, based upon the conviction that Jesus was God's Messiah, His agent to transform the world. In Capernaum He exorcised evil spirits, healed the sick and astounded the crowds with the authority by which He spoke. Soon His reputation spread far and wide.

In Galilee, Jesus ascended a mountain, sat down and taught His disciples and others who overheard His famous "Sermon on the Mount." In those inspired words He laid out His agenda, His vision for the Kingdom of God. Many followed Him in discipleship in addition to those twelve whom He chose.

As Jesus continued to travel throughout Galilee, He taught in parables about the Kingdom of God. Many heard Him speak, and they believed in the good news. Others considered Him a blasphemer. They criticized Him for violating Sabbath law and breaking with the traditions handed down to them. According to some, Jesus associated with sinners and was a sinner himself. His opponents began to plot against Him.

Jesus continued to do miracles and gave His disciples authority to act in his stead. While in Capernaum, He called the twelve together and sent them on a mission to proclaim the Kingdom of God in villages and homes that would receive them. He gave them power over disease and evil spirits. Near Bethsaida, thousands came to hear Jesus teach and perhaps see some miracles. Late in the day they would see a miracle when Jesus divided the loaves and fishes and fed over five thousand. According to the historian Josephus about this time John the Baptist sat in Herod Antipas' prison at Machaerus, a fortress on the eastern side of the Dead Sea. In his discouragement, John sent messengers to Jesus and asked Him if He was the Messiah after all. Jesus sent the messengers back to John, telling them to report that the blind see, the lame walk, the lepers are cleansed, the deaf hear, the dead are raised and the poor hear the good news. Not long afterwards Herod had John beheaded.

When the crowds' demands became too heavy upon Jesus, He would withdraw for seasons of privacy and meditation. Once He and His disciples traveled to Caesarea Philippi. Along the way He asked His disciples to consider who He was. Peter, speaking for the company, confessed, "You are the Messiah, the Son of the living God" (Matt. 16:16). With this Jesus said that He must go to Jerusalem. There He would suffer and die, but on the third day He would be raised. Several times Jesus predicted His crucifixion and resurrection, but His disciples never seemed to hear or understand what He was saying.

When it became clear that His Galilean ministry had ended, Jesus set His face to go to Jerusalem for the last time. On the way He did not travel through Samaria as was His custom. Instead He crossed the Jordan and ministered in the region of Perea. There He encountered a rich man who wanted to know the path to eternal life. Jesus instructed him to sell all He had and give it to the poor. Then He crossed over the Jordan and passed through Jericho towards Jerusalem.

Jesus entered Jerusalem on a Sunday. He rode a donkey, amid shouts of "Hosanna! Blessed is the one who comes in the name of the Lord! Blessed is the coming kingdom of our ancestor David!" (Mark 11:9-10). Apparently, the crowds now believed Him to be the Messiah; and they wished Him to declare it openly during the festival of Passover. During Jesus' last week, He entered the temple and drove out those religious officials who were accused of robbing the worshippers. He enacted parables and spoke clearly how one day the temple would be destroyed. Indeed, in less than forty years the Second Temple would lie in ruins, a casualty of Roman aggression and vengeance.

On Thursday, Jesus and His disciples sat down to eat the Passover feast in the Upper Room. As the evening progressed, the Lord took the bread and the cup and blessed and distributed them to his followers with these words of institution: "this is my body" (Mark 14:22) and "this is my blood of the covenant, which is poured out for many" (Mark 14:24). He asked His disciples to remember this meal and to rehearse it whenever they gathered together. As the evening wore on, Jesus instructed His disciples and prayed for them. Although they did not know what was happening, they sensed His anxiety and growing pain. Then they left the Upper Room and came to Gethsemane, one of Jesus' favorite places. There Jesus agonized and prayed while His disciples slept. He pled with God for another path but resigned His will to the plan of the Father. Not long after, Judas Iscariot, one of the twelve, arrived accompanied by a detachment of soldiers that took Jesus into custody.

According to the New Testament, back in Jerusalem, the Sanhedrin gathered to examine Jesus. Witnesses came forward to accuse Him but ultimately His own words condemned Him of blasphemy. The religious leaders decided to send Jesus to Pilate, the Roman governor. They claimed Jesus desired to be made King of the Jews. In his headquarters Pilate interviewed Jesus but found no substance to the charges. The Gospels tell us that Jesus' opponents instigated the crowd to call for His execution. Pilate gave the decision to the crowd and ordered Jesus to be crucified.

Early Friday morning Jesus carried His cross through the streets of Jerusalem. Onlookers sympathized with Him but could do nothing against the might of the Roman presence. They led Him to a hill outside the city called Golgotha ("the place of the skull"), and there they crucified Him between two thieves. A sign above the cross said it all: "The King of the Jews." By noon darkness enshrouded the land. By three o'clock in the afternoon Jesus cried to God in the words of Psalm 22 (Matt. 27:46): "My God, my God, why have you forsaken me?" In a few minutes He breathed His last and gave up His spirit to God.

One of the council members, Joseph of Arimathea, asked Pilate for the body of Jesus. He wished to bury it with dignity according to Jewish custom. Pilate allowed it, and so Joseph purchased linen and arranged for Jesus' body to be placed in a new tomb not far from where He was crucified.

On the first day of the week, Mary Magdalene and some other women went to the tomb to anoint the body of Jesus. But when they arrived, the stone sealing the tomb had been rolled away and Jesus' body was gone. A man dressed in a white robe told them that Jesus had been resurrected. He instructed them to tell the disciples what had happened; and so the good news of His resurrection began to spread. Some did not believe until they saw the risen Jesus face-to-face. Others seemed to believe without needing any proof. The risen Lord continued to appear to His disciples in Judea as well as in Galilee, convincing them that He had indeed conquered death.

On the Mount of Olives Jesus appeared to His disciples and instructed them to stay in Jerusalem until God's promise had been fulfilled. He said that they would receive power when the Holy Spirit descended upon them and that they would be witnesses in Jerusalem, Judea, Samaria, even to the ends of the earth (Acts 1:8). As He said these words, He ascended into heaven with the promise that He would come again.

Written by Rev. David B. Capes, Ph.D

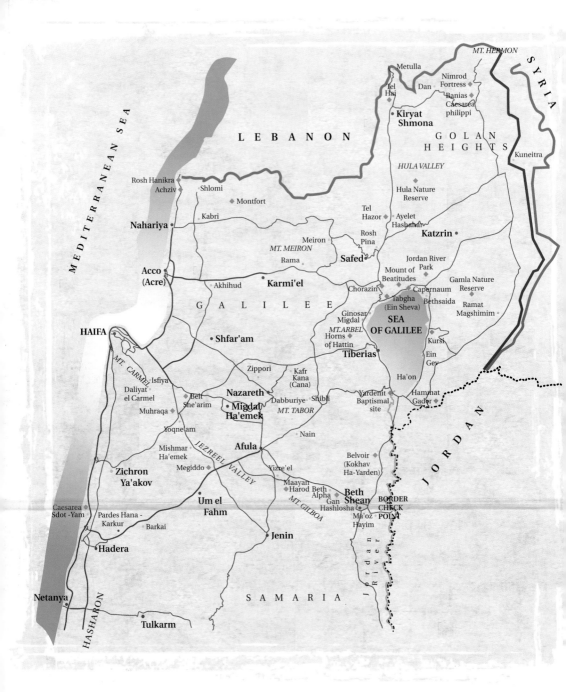

Galilee

Sea of Galilee

Golan Heights

Northern Valleys

Northern Coast

Mount Carmel

Mount Gilboa

10

Jesus
in the Northern Regions
of the Holy Land

The northern regions of the Holy Land flow with many streams, contain rich vegetation and are filled with a host of hidden, natural treasures. They offer numerous archaeological sites and exciting views. During much of the year they are covered by a carpet of flowers, a rainbow of colors when in full bloom. These regions contain much of the Holy Land's fresh water. The heavy precipitation which usually falls here runs off into the Jordan River and fills the Sea of Galilee.

In the middle of the region sits the "Jewel in the crown," the focus of tourist interest, the Sea of Galilee. The basalt Golan Heights and the lofty peak of Mount Hermon rise to the east. The beautiful, charming landscapes of Galilee extend west to the Mediterranean Sea. Hiding between the mountains are the fertile Hula Valley and the Jordan River.

Southwest of the region is Mount Carmel on the coast, with the city of Haifa. South of the northern region rises Mount Gilboa with its special vistas. The Jezreel Valley and other smaller valleys connect them with an intricate network of fields.

It was in the Holy Land's northern regions that Jesus lived most of his life. His parents raised and educated him here. According to the Gospels, he began his public ministry in these hills. Visitors to these regions can see all of those special sites where Jesus taught his followers about the Kingdom of Heaven, healed the sick, fed the multitudes and performed other miracles.

As a whole, Galilee and its environs offer tourists a wide range of attractions which will educate, refresh and entertain. In addition to its ample antiquities, museums, and city tours, there are hiking tours, horse - or donkey-back tours and jeep tours. The rivers and beaches of the north provide an assortment of water sports. The northern regions also offer special accommodations with a quiet atmosphere. Guests can stay in private homes, rent small houses or experience the communal life of a kibbutz.

Nazareth

In the sixth month the angel Gabriel was sent by God to a town in Galilee called Nazareth, to a virgin engaged to a man whose name was Joseph, of the house of David. The virgin's name was Mary. And he came to her and said, "Greetings, favored one! The Lord is with you." . . . [The angel continued] "Do not be afraid, Mary, for you have found favor with God. And now, you will conceive in your womb and bear a son, and you will name him Jesus. He will be great, and will be called the Son of the Most High, and the Lord God will give to him the throne of his ancestor David. He will reign over the house of Jacob forever, and of his kingdom there will be no end." . . . Then Mary said, "Here am I, the servant of the Lord; let it be with me according to your word." Then the angel departed from her.

Luke 1:26-38

The Basilica of the Annunciation

Interior of the Church of the Annunciation

The altar in the Holy Grotto

Nazareth, the "City of the Annunciation," is the city of Mary, the Virgin Mother of Jesus. In this town, the angel Gabriel revealed to Mary the imminent birth of Jesus and John the Baptist. It is the place where Jesus *"increased in wisdom and in years"* (Luke 2:52). Here Jesus learned the trade of a carpenter. Later, in his public ministry, he returned to Nazareth and read from the prophet Isaiah in his famous synagogue sermon: *"'The Spirit of the Lord is upon me, because he has anointed me to bring good news to the poor. He has sent me to proclaim release to the captives and recovery of sight to the blind,* to let the oppressed go free, to proclaim the year of the Lord's favor'"* (Luke 4:18-19). Initially the people spoke well of him and were amazed at his gracious wisdom. But soon it became clear that *"no prophet is accepted in the prophet's hometown....They [the townspeople] got up, drove him out of the town, and led him to the brow of the hill . . . so that they might hurl him off the cliff. But he passed through the midst of them and went on his way"* (Luke 4:29-30).

The Church of the Annunciation (Catholic) is said to be built over the place where Gabriel appeared to Mary to announce that she would be the Savior's mother. It is one of the largest and most magnificent churches in the Holy Land. The new structure, dedicated in 1969, is built on two levels in order to integrate and preserve the ancient site.

On the lower level is the **Holy Grotto**, surrounded by what remains of the Byzantine and Crusader churches. (In the eighteenth century the Franciscan order renovated the structure.) On the upper level is the new modern church, its huge cupola hovering above the holy cave. The modern basilica contains a wealth of art intended to enhance the splendor of the place. Many mosaics, all dedicated to honoring the Virgin Mary, grace the walls of the church hall. These have been donated by different Christian communities throughout the world.

Nazareth lies in a lovely setting in the middle of Galilee range. Pilgrims called it the "Flower of the Galilee," for the surrounding mountains enclose it like petals around a flower.

Mary's Well in the center of Nazareth

Beneath the floor of the Byzantine church, archaeologists discovered some remains of the ancient city of Nazareth, including houses, granaries, cells for storing wine or oil and pottery. Caves and other relics were found, used apparently in later periods for religious rituals. On the walls of the caves pilgrims have left their mark in drawings and graffiti. One of the inscriptions reads, "XE MAPIA," Greek for "HAIL MARY," the first words spoken by Gabriel to Mary at the Annunciation (Luke 1:28).

Nearby stands the **Church of St. Joseph** (Franciscan). According to tradition, it is built over the site of Joseph's workshop. There Joseph would have taught Jesus the trade of a carpenter. The lower level of the church contains a water reservoir hewn out of the rock, a granary cave and a pit.

In the center of the city is **Mary's Well**. At one time it may have been the only source of water available to the city.

An aqueduct carried water from the spring to the well. The townspeople would have gathered there to draw water into their vessels. It is likely that Mary and Jesus came here to draw and drink from these waters.

Near Mary's Well stands the **Church of St. Gabriel** (Greek Orthodox). The church is located above the spring which tourists can hear gurgling as they approach the church. According to one tradition, the Archangel Gabriel appeared to Mary when she was drawing water from the fountain. The church was built over the remains of earlier churches, the first one erected by the Crusaders. It was renovated by the Greek Orthodox in the eighteenth century.

Nazareth contains many other churches and monasteries. Some have been built on the sites of ancient churches from the Byzantine and Crusader eras.

The Church of St. Gabriel

The Church of the Synagogue is dedicated to the sabbath sermon Jesus preached in Nazareth at the beginning of his public ministry (Luke 4:16-27). **The Basilica of Jesus the Adolescent**, which sits on a northern hill of Nazareth, has an impressive view of the town below. It also has attractive architecture and a lovely statue of Jesus as an adolescent. It is maintained by the French Salesian Order.

Another site commemorates the place where Jesus miraculously disappeared from the eyes of the angry townspeople (Luke 4:28-30).

In the center of the city stands the **"Old-New Market,"** the hub of commercial activity. The market contains a variety of interesting shops interspersed with specialty grocery stores that sell such items as olive oil, unusual spices, goat's cheese ("Labane") and other items produced in Galilee.

The Village of Cana

On the third day there was a wedding in Cana of Galilee . . . When the wine gave out, the mother of Jesus said to him, "They have no wine.". . . Now standing there were six stone water jars for the Jewish rites of purification, each holding twenty or thirty gallons. Jesus said to them, "Fill the jars with water." And they filled them up to the brim. He said to them, "Now draw some out, and take it to the chief steward." So they took it. When the steward tasted the water that had become wine, and did not know where it came from, . . . the steward called to the bridegroom and said to him, "Everyone serves the good wine first, . . . But you have kept the good wine until now."

John 2:1-10

The Gospel of John states that Jesus performed his first public miracle in Cana of Galilee. He performed a second "sign" here as well when he cured the royal official's son who lay sick in Capernaum (John 4:46-54). Nathanael, one of the twelve, called Cana his hometown (John 21:2).

Situated on the road between Nazareth and Tiberias, the present Arab village Kafr Kana rests today on the ruins of ancient Cana. Olive groves and pomegranate orchards, known for their high-quality produce, surround

The Greek Orthodox Church of Cana

The Franciscan Church of Cana

this picturesque village. In the center of the village flows a spring which was once the main source of water for the people who lived here. The steeples of the churches stand erect above the houses and serve as a constant reminder of the significance of this place for the story of Jesus.

Sunset in Kafr Kana

The Sea of Galilee

As Jesus passed along the Sea of Galilee, he saw Simon and his brother Andrew casting a net into the sea--for they were fishermen. And Jesus said to them, "Follow me and I will make you fish for people." And immediately they left their nets and followed him.

Mark 1:16-18

When he saw that they were straining at the oars against an adverse wind, he came towards them early in the morning, walking on the sea. He intended to pass them by. But when they saw him walking on the sea, they thought it was a ghost and cried out; for they all saw him and were terrified. But immediately he spoke to them and said, "Take heart, it is I; do not be afraid."

Mark 6:48-50

The Sea of Galilee and the fertile valleys surrounding it are like an earthly Garden of Eden. It is not by chance that these scenic shores provide the backdrop for so many important events in the life of Jesus. By its waters he chose his first disciples, healed the sick and preached the gospel of the Kingdom. The Gospels record that Jesus walked on the Sea of Galilee to join his disciples in a boat (Matt. 14:22-33). When on another occasion he spoke to a storm to calm the wind and waves, his disciples wondered: *"'Who then is this, that even the wind and the sea obey him?'"* (Mark 4:35-41).

The many authors of the Bible refer to the Sea of Galilee under several names. In the Old Testament it is called the sea of Chinnereth or Chinneroth (Numb. 34:11; Josh. 12:3), perhaps for the town of the same name that once lay on the northwestern coast. The archaeological excavation of **Tel Kinnerot (Chinnereth)** sheds some light on the ancient people who lived there. In the New Testament John refers to it as the Sea of Tiberias (John 6:1) while Luke calls it the lake of Gennesaret (Luke 5:1). The Hebrew name of the Sea today is lake Kinneret.

Because of its fresh water and excellent fishing, the Sea of Galilee has attracted generations of settlers to its shores. Archaeologists have discovered that prehistoric tribes once lived in this region.

Excavations of jetties and port facilities have provided evidence that boating and fishing industries thrived around the Sea.

The Sea of Galilee is 22 km (13 miles) long by 12 km (7 miles) wide. It lies approximately 210 m (675 feet) below sea level.

Today, in addition to being the main source of fresh water for Israel, the Sea of Galilee serves as a center for tourism. Resort facilities on its banks provide a wide variety of holiday choices. On the northern end where the Jordan River meets the sea the **Jordan River (Ha-Yarden) Park** is located. It contains recreational facilities including a picnic area and water sports. It also boasts the remains of aqueducts built to supply water for nearby flour mills. Clearly, modern Israel has left its mark on the Sea of Galilee. Located on the southern shore is **Bet Gabriel**, a cultural center famous for its exquisite architecture against the backdrop of the sea and the mountains.

The Jordan River
Yardenit Baptismal Site

The Jordan River runs from the northern region of the Holy Land through the Sea of Galilee on its way south to the Dead Sea. Originating at the foot of Mount Hermon, the river collects three streams to its water: The Dan, Snir (Hatzbani) and Hermon (Banias). These bodies of water are parts of a great fissure, the Syrian-African Rift, the deepest land rift in the world.

On the northern end of the Sea of Galilee, where the Jordan River meets the sea, the Jordan River Park is located.

[John the Baptist said,] "I baptize you with water for repentance, but one who is more powerful than I is coming after me; I am not worthy to carry his sandals. He will baptize you with the Holy Spirit and fire."
Matthew 3:11

Now when all the people were baptized, and when Jesus also had been baptized and was praying, the heaven was opened, and the Holy Spirit descended upon him in bodily from like a dove. And a voice came from heaven, "You are my Son, the Beloved; with you I am well pleased."
Luke 3:21-22

Along the Jordan River, John the Baptist preached a baptism of repentance for the forgiveness of sins. His ministry culminated with the baptism of Jesus of Nazareth.

Pilgrims to the Holy Land can visit the Baptismal site of Yardenit, at the point where the Jordan River flows out of the Sea of Galilee, and be baptized in the waters of the Jordan.

Scenes from the Yardenit baptismal site on the southern end of the Sea of Galilee

Capernaum

Now when Jesus heard that John had been arrested, he withdrew to Galilee. He left Nazareth and made his home in Capernaum by the sea . . .

Matthew 4:12-13

Capernaum played a pivotal role in the life of Jesus. After his baptism and John's arrest he chose to live there and to make it his headquarters of ministry. Matthew and Mark refer to Capernaum as Jesus' hometown. From here he would travel and preach his gospel of the Kingdom to cities and villages throughout Galilee.

In Capernaum he called disciples (Matt. 9:9), befriended tax collectors, healed the sick (e.g., Mark 2:1-12) and preached to the multitudes. On a sabbath day in Capernaum's synagogue Jesus captivated his audience with his teaching, his authority and his ability to cast out evil spirits (Luke 4:31-37).

Perhaps the greatest miracle Jesus performed in Capernaum was the raising of Jairus' daughter: *"When they came to the house of the leader of the synagogue, . . . he said to them, 'Why do you make a commotion and weep? The child is not dead but sleeping.' . . . He took her by the* hand and said to her, 'Talitha cum,' which means, 'Little girl, get up!' And immediately the girl got up and began to walk about"* (Mark 5:38-42).

Nevertheless, despite Jesus' ministry and the miracles he performed there, in the end he prophesied bitterness and destruction for this seaside town:

Capernaum Synagogue

And you, Capernaum, will you be exalted to heaven?

No, you will be brought down to Hades.

For if the deeds of power done in you had been done in Sodom, it would have remained until this day. But I tell you that on the day of judgment it will be more tolerable for the land of Sodom than for you."

Matthew 11:23-24

Capernaum, located on the north-western shore of the Sea of Galilee, is not mentioned in the Old Testament, but it was a place of importance in the time of the New Testament. It is mentioned also in Josephus' documents from the first century A.D. and is identified with "Kefar Nahum" of later Jewish literature. The village flourished uninterrupted until the Arab period in the seventh and eighth centuries A.D. Later it became a small fishing village.

A frieze depicting a temple carried on a chariot, found in Capernaum.

In the middle of the area, archaeologists unearthed the remains of an elaborate synagogue. Next to it is a dwelling which could be the home of St. Peter. These are surrounded by the remains of other houses and agricultural installations.

The Capernaum Synagogue was built on an elevated area in the center of the settlement. The splendid building was made of large carved limestone blocks brought from afar which contrast dramatically with the local basalt rocks. The synagogue was built in the Byzantine period over the remains of an earlier first century A.D. building. (Some scholars identify additional strata from the third century.) Among the remains, archaeologists found many stones covered with engravings of typical Jewish motifs, such as the Menorah (a seven-branched candlestick). They also found an engraving of a temple on a wheeled chariot, which may be interpreted as a movable Ark of the Law.

Ruins of the ancient synagogue of Capernaum

Opposite page: An aerial view of Capernaum

The archaeological site of St. Peter's House

The House of St. Peter underwent many changes over the years. The original foundation served as a private house from the first century B.C. In the fourth century A.D. the structure was separated from the rest of the town by a wall and renovated with elaborate decorations. In the fifth century an octagonal church was built over the earlier structures. The facility contains many inscriptions in different languages in praise of Jesus and St. Peter.

In order to preserve the site, a modern church was recently built directly over it. It rests on eight pillars and has an octagonal shape just like the original church. The Franciscans oversee the church and all the archaeological excavations around it.

Just east of this site is the **Greek Orthodox Church.** It is distinguished by several beautiful domes which complement the church's architecture and contrast splendidly with the mountains and the Sea of Galilee.

Church of the Beatitudes

The Sermon on the Mount

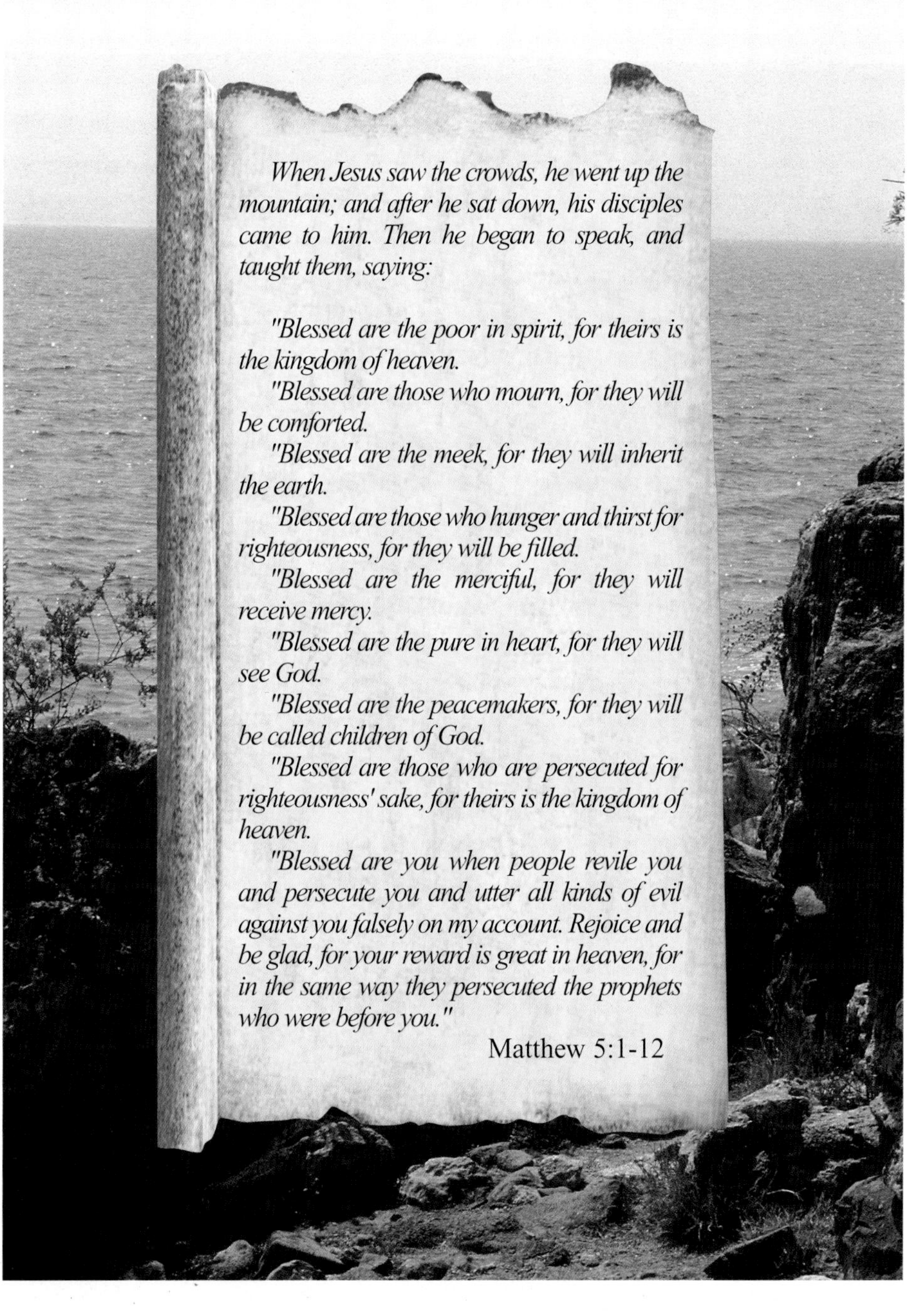

When Jesus saw the crowds, he went up the mountain; and after he sat down, his disciples came to him. Then he began to speak, and taught them, saying:

"Blessed are the poor in spirit, for theirs is the kingdom of heaven.

"Blessed are those who mourn, for they will be comforted.

"Blessed are the meek, for they will inherit the earth.

"Blessed are those who hunger and thirst for righteousness, for they will be filled.

"Blessed are the merciful, for they will receive mercy.

"Blessed are the pure in heart, for they will see God.

"Blessed are the peacemakers, for they will be called children of God.

"Blessed are those who are persecuted for righteousness' sake, for theirs is the kingdom of heaven.

"Blessed are you when people revile you and persecute you and utter all kinds of evil against you falsely on my account. Rejoice and be glad, for your reward is great in heaven, for in the same way they persecuted the prophets who were before you."

Matthew 5:1-12

33

The Mount of Beatitudes

From this beautiful spot, north of the Sea of Galilee, above the springs of Tabgha, Jesus gave his most famous address, the Sermon on the Mount. Today, a Catholic church, monastery and hostel stand here, surrounded by well-manicured gardens. The church was built in 1936-8. It was designed by Barluzzi who took special pride in its architecture. The building is octagonal to represent the eight Beatitudes from the Sermon on the Mount. Symbols around the altar recall the attributes of a disciple which Jesus said would make one blessed.

On the mount there is an incredible vantage point overlooking the Sea of Galilee. Not far away, on the slopes of a hill, one can see the ruins of the ancient church dedicated to the Sermon on the Mount.

Horns of Hattin and Mount Arbel

The Horns of Hattin and Mount Arbel overlook the western shore of the Sea of Galilee.

The Horns of Hattin is so named because its two peaks resemble horns. It became famous due to an important battle between the Crusaders and the Muslims which took place on the slopes of the mountain in 1187. In that clash Saladin defeated the Crusaders, effectively bringing to an end the Crusader Kingdom of Jerusalem.

There is one Christian tradition that Jesus gave his famous Sermon on the Mount from a hill next to the Horns of Hattin, but not many accept this view.

On one slope of the mountain, guests can visit a site holy to the Druze. Called in Arabic "Nebi Shu'ayb," it is said to contain the tomb of the prophet Jethro, the father-in-law of Moses.

Mount Arbel (also known as **Mount Nittai)** may be best known for its impressive cliff leading down to the shoreline of the Sea of Galilee. Caverns, caves and the remains of several fortifications and castles mark the cliff. The historian Josephus relates how Jewish zealots fortified themselves in the caves of "Arbela." To attack them King Herod's soldiers reached the caves by throwing ropes from above (*Jewish War* 1.309-313). In Jewish literature from the sixth and seventh centuries A.D., the Valley of Arbel is mentioned as the place where redemption would begin following a battle there. On the summit of the mount, archaeological excavations have revealed a large synagogue with several strata dating from the Roman and the Byzantine periods.

Above: Trail-rides throughout Galilee with
"Vered Hagalil"
Below: Horns of Hattin

The cliff of Mount Arbel leading to the Sea of Galilee.

⊤he Ancient Boat

One of the most intriguing finds from the time of Jesus is an ancient boat found in the Sea of Galilee. The boat sank nearly two thousand years ago. When it was discovered, it was in an advanced state of disintegration. Today after much work to restore the boat, it is on display (with the permission of the Israel Antiquities Authority) in the educational center of Kibbutz Ginosar, **Beth Yigal Allon**, **Man in the Galilee Museum.**

The center introduces visitors to Galilee as an area of unique landscapes and a wealth of history; it also focuses on the settlements today. The center is dedicated to Yigal Allon, who was both an important political and military leader in Israel.

M igdal
(Magdala)

On the western shore of the Sea of Galilee sits the modern village of Migdal. This village is near the ancient town of Magdala, the hometown of Mary Magdalene. According to the Gospels, Mary Magdalene became a devoted disciple of Jesus. Along with some other women she helped to support his ministry (Luke 8:1-3). In Jerusalem, she stood near his cross and watched his burial (Mark 15:40). She was one of the first to come to the tomb after his resurrection and the first to see the Risen Lord (John 20:1-18).

Soon afterwards he went on through cities and villages, proclaiming and bringing the good news of the kingdom of God. The twelve were with him, as well as some women who had been cured of evil spirits and infirmities: Mary, called Magdalene, from whom seven demons had gone out . . .
Luke 8:1-2

The original town of Magdala lay at the crossing of the roads between Nazareth and the Sea of Galilee next to the cliffs of Mount Arbel. According to the historian Josephus, it was a large town during the Second Temple period. During a marine excavation archaeologists found the remains of the harbor of ancient Migdal. This harbor apparently was the base for the Jewish Navy during the Jewish Revolt (A.D. 66-70).

K ursi

Then they arrived at the country of the Gerasenes, which is opposite Galilee. As he stepped out on land, a man of the city who had demons met him. . . . When he saw Jesus, he fell down before him and shouted at top of his voice, "What have you to do with me, Jesus, Son of the Most High God? I beg you, Do not torment me.". . . Now there on the hillside a large herd of swine was feeding; and the demons begged Jesus to let them enter these. So he gave them permission. Then the demons came out of the man and entered the swine, and the herd rushed down the steep bank into the lake and was drowned.

Luke 8:26-33

The traditional site for Jesus' encounter with the man who had the legion of demons is known today as Kursi. (In the New Testament the Gospels name the place differently: Matthew calls it the country of the Gadarenes; Mark and Luke call it the country of the Gerasenes).

Located on the eastern shore of the Sea of Galilee, visitors to Kursi can see the remains of an impressive monastery and church built in the fifth century A.D. A high wall surrounded it, encompassing residential units, public buildings and agricultural installations. A street paved with basalt slabs led from the main gate of the enclosure to the church. The church, built in the basilica style, is adorned with mosaics of local flora and fauna. A Greek inscription found at the entrance to the baptistery indicates that its floor was paved in A.D. 585 and was dedicated by Stephanus, head of the monastery.

On the slope of the nearest cliff, southeast to the monastery, excavations exposed the remains of a square tower and a small chapel. The topographical conditions of the site of these remains are similar to those described in the Gospel accounts of the meeting between Jesus and the man who was possessed by demons.

Bethsaida and Chorazin

Jesus pronounced "Woe!" against Chorazin and Bethsaida because their citizens refused to follow his teachings, despite the miracles he performed in their midst. Two other cities, Tyre and Sidon, will fare better on judgment day than these towns. According to Matthew 15:21, Jesus traveled north to these cities--located on the coast of modern Lebanon.

In **Korazim National Park**, north of Capernaum, one can see the remains of the ancient Jewish town of Chorazin. According to the excavations the town's shape conforms to the topography of the hill on which it was built. The central quarter of the town contains a synagogue and several large buildings in its vicinity.

Ancient synagogue in Korazim National Park

The excavations of **Bethsaida** are located in Bik'at Beit Saida Reserve (the plain of Bethsaida), on the northeast shore of the Sea of Galilee. The streams that flow from the Golan Heights to the Sea of Galilee slow down here and create a wide and multibranched delta with a large variety of flora and fauna.

The excavation site of Bethsaida

39

Tabgha (Ein Sheva)

The Fertile Tabgha spreads along the north-western shore of the Sea of Galilee. Its name comes from the Greek "Heptapegon," which means "seven springs," but has been corrupted into the Arabic name, Tabgha.

According to tradition, some of the more significant events in Jesus' ministry took place in this area. He multiplied the loaves and fish here. On a nearby mountain, he gave his Sermon on the Mount. Following his resurrection, he appeared to his disciples along the shore and appointed Simon Peter to his place of leadership in the early church.

The area of Tabgha
Right: The Church of the Primacy of St. Peter
Inset: The Church of the Feeding of the Multitude

The Multiplication of the Loaves and Fish

> Then he ordered the crowds to sit down on the grass. Taking the five loaves and the two fish, he looked up to heaven, and blessed and broke the loaves, and gave them to the disciples, and the disciples gave them to the crowds. And all ate and were filled, and they took up what was left over of the broken pieces, twelve baskets full. And those who ate were about five thousand men, besides women and children.
>
> Matthew 14:19-21

In Tabgha, on the northwestern shore of the Sea of Galilee, within a beautiful garden stands the Catholic **Church of the First Feeding of the Multitude**.

The original church was built in the Byzantine era in several phases and modified in later centuries. The church contains one of the most beautiful mosaic floors ever discovered in the Holy Land. Perhaps its most striking symbols—located at the top of the mosaic under the altar—are the loaves flanked by two fish commemorating Jesus' miracle performed here.

In A.D. 614 the church was destroyed in the Persian invasion. The new basilica was constructed on the ancient foundations of the church, preserving its style and incorporating all antique elements that had been found. It is operated today under the auspices of Benedictine monks.

The Byzantine mosaic of the loaves and fish

"And immediately he got into the boat with his disciples and went to the district of Dalmanutha."

Mark 8:10

Tiberias

Situated on the western shore, Tiberias remains the largest settlement around the Sea of Galilee. King Herod Antipas, the son of Herod the Great, established the city and named it in honor of the Roman emperor Tiberius who ruled from A.D. 14-37. Under his reign Pontius Pilate was appointed governor of Judea. The city was extended and in the third century it was granted the status of a Roman colony, as coins from the era clearly indicate.

From a Jewish perspective, Tiberias carries significance as one of four sacred cities (the others are Jerusalem, Hebron and Safed). During the second and third centuries, Tiberias became known as a center for Jewish studies. The Sanhedrin, the Jewish council, moved from Zippori (Sepphoris) to Tiberias. Many famous sages lived in Tiberias. Much of the commentary on the Mishnah (the Jewish oral laws) known as the Jerusalem or Palestinian Talmud, was written in Tiberias as well. Today, in this area one finds the traditional burial places of such famous Jewish rabbis as Maimonides, Rabbi Meir and Rabbi Akiba.

Alongside the Jewish community lived a Christian community. Throughout the ages, especially in the Byzantine and Crusader eras, several churches were built in the area. One of the Crusader churches was dedicated to St. Peter. The Franciscan order restored it and continues to care for it today. Tiberias contains other churches and monasteries like the Greek Orthodox monastery and the Church of Scotland.

Wooden sailing boat which is similar to the ancient boats, "HOLYLAND SAILING ," on the Sea of Galilee, Tiberias.

The ancient city's western boundary was marked by Mount Berenice which still offers a spectacular view of Tiberias and the Sea of Galilee. On the Mount archaeologists found remains of fortifications and administrative buildings from the Roman period and churches from later periods.

In 1033 Tiberias was destroyed by an earthquake. The city was later rebuilt by the Crusaders, who moved the site to the north, its present location.

In the southern sectors of Tiberias, the ancient **Hammath-Tiberias** contains hot springs and an archaeological site. For many centuries, the hot springs were sought for their medicinal and healing qualities. Today, visitors may enjoy a spa and a recreational center.

Nearby, archaeologists excavated several synagogues dating from the fourth to the eighth centuries. They uncovered a unique mosaic floor that once decorated one of the synagogues. Though it has faded, it is evident that it was extremely colorful. It contains inscriptions and a wheel with the signs of the Zodiac beside such Jewish symbols as the Torah Ark and the Menorah.

With its beautiful beachfront properties, its luxury hotels and its restaurants, Tiberias today is a popular vacation and holiday destination.

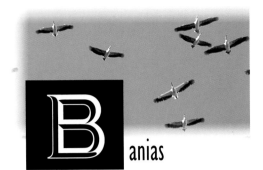

Banias
Caesarea Philippi

Jesus traveled as far north as Caesarea Philippi, the present day Banias, in the southern foothills of Mount Hermon. From the area flow springs which feed into the Banias Stream, one of the sources of the Jordan River. The Greeks referred to it as Paneas after the nature-cult god Pan. Pagans performed his rites in the caverns near the source of the springs. The Arabs corrupted the Greek "Paneas" to "Banias," its current name.

In the first century B.C. Herod the Great built a temple here in honor of Caesar Augustus. Herod's son, Philip, while tetrarch of the region, constructed the city and named it Caesarea Philippi.

Though most famous as the site of Peter's confession of Jesus' messiahship, some traditions also hold that the woman who suffered from hemorrhages for twelve years and was healed by Jesus in Capernaum (Mark 5:24-34) came from Caesarea Philippi. One tradition holds that Jesus' transfiguration (Matt. 17:1-8) happened nearby.

The Christian community in this area was well established by the early fourth century and churches were erected. Its importance increased in the Middle Ages, as a prosperous city on the road to Damascus. Most of the archaeological remains of the city from all its periods can be found near the source of the springs.

> Now when Jesus came into the district of Caesarea Philippi, he asked his disciples, "Who do people say that the Son of Man is?" And they said, "Some say John the Baptist, but others Elijah, and still others Jeremiah or one of the prophets." He said to them, "But who do you say that I am?" Simon Peter answered, "You are the Messiah, the Son of the living God." And Jesus answered him, "Blessed are you, Simon son of Jonah! For flesh and blood has not revealed this to you, but my Father in heaven...."
>
> Matthew 16:13-17

M ount Hermon

Mount Hermon with its white-capped summit rises in the north of the Holy Land, above the Hula Valley and the Golan Heights. It extends north-east to the regions of Lebanon and Syria.

Mount Hermon is referred to in the Old Testament as a blessed mountain and has been regarded as such since ancient times. *"Tabor and Hermon joyously praise your name"* (Psalms 89:12). The peak of the mountain was considered sacred in antiquity. In ancient times shrines and temples sat atop it.

According to one tradition Mount Hermon was the Mount of the Transfiguration of Jesus (Matt. 17:1-8).

Below: Mount Hermon
Right: North of Banias and south to the Hermon Mountain lies Nimrod Fortress. One of the largest and best preserved castles from the Crusader period.

The written sources and the archaeological finds from Mount Hermon indicate that despite the harsh climate, plentiful precipitation, heavy snows and strong winds, some settlements did exist on the mount. The archaeological excavations include finds from the Hellenistic, Roman, Byzantine and Medieval periods.

Mount Hermon is today the only ski resort in Israel during the winter season. It includes a holiday resort village on the slopes and facilities for skiing.

The Transfiguration of Jesus

Six days later, Jesus took with him Peter and James and his brother John and led them up a high mountain, by themselves. And he was transfigured before them, and his face shone like the sun, and his clothes became dazzling white. Suddenly there appeared to them Moses and Elijah, talking with him. Then Peter said to Jesus, "Lord, it is good for us to be here; if you wish, I will make three dwellings here, one for you, one for Moses, and one for Elijah." While he was still speaking, suddenly a bright cloud overshadowed them, and from the cloud a voice said, "This is my Son, the Beloved; with him I am well pleased; listen to him!"

Matthew 17 :1- 5

Mount Tabor

Mount Tabor, with its beautiful and peculiar dome shape, rises majestically in Galilee. From its summit visitors experience a breathtaking view of the surrounding area. Due to its rich ever-green vegetation the mount appears green throughout the year.

The height and location of Mount Tabor made it a strategic asset in all the battles fought in the area. In one of the most famous battles Deborah, the prophetess and judge, and Barak waged war against Sisera and the Canaanites. Barak and the Israelites took position at Mount Tabor and swept down towards Sisera, the com-mander of Jabin's army. At the end of the battle *"Sisera got down from his chariot and fled away on foot . . . All the army of Sisera fell by the sword; no one was left"* (Judg. 4:15-16).

Since the early Byzantine period, a Christian tradition developed that the summit of Mount Tabor was the site of Jesus' transfiguration. At the summit of the mount several churches were erected during the Byzantine and the Crusader periods. The modern **Church of the Transfiguration** was dedicated by the Franciscan order in 1925. They incorporated the new construction with the remains of previous churches. The church contains an exquisite mosaic depicting the transfigured Jesus between Moses and Elijah, rep-resentatives of the Law and the Prophets. Two chapels, one dedicated to Moses, the other to Elijah, make up the unique structure.

Near the Basilica are the ruins of a large church and monastery from the Crusader era. During the time of the Crusades Mount Tabor became a place of strategic military importance. Standing today are the ruins of the fortifications and walls erected during this period.

Close by, the **Chapel of the Descent** commemorates Jesus' instructions to his disciples not to tell what they had seen until after his resurrection (Mark 9:9).

On the northern part of the summit stands the **Church of St. Elijah** and its monastery under the auspices of the Greek Orthodox Church. In the vicinity is the **Cave of Melchizedek** where, according to one tradition, the priest-king received and blessed Abraham (Gen. 14:17-20).

At the western base of the mount sits the Arab village of **Dabburiye**, which may be the place where Jesus healed the youth stricken with epilepsy (Matt. 17:14-21). Jesus' other disciples likely waited here when their Master ascended the mountain with Peter, James and John.

Just south of Mt. Tabor is the Arab village of **Nain** were tradition holds that Jesus entered and saw the funeral procession of a young man. The Lord felt compassion for the widow and resuscitated her son to the delight of all (Luke 7:11-17).

At the northern base of Mount Tabor sits the Bedouin village of **Shibli. The Galilee Bedouin Heritage Center** is located here. Guests to this center can enjoy the hospitality and culture of these people. When you hear the Bedouin men pound the coffee beans, you know that it is time to enter the tents, enjoy the brew and listen to the stories they tell.

Church of the Transfiguration, Mount Tabor

The Primacy of St. Peter

When they had finished break-fast, Jesus said to Simon Peter, "Simon son of John, do you love me more than these?" He said to him, "Yes, Lord; you know that I love you." Jesus said to him, "Feed my lambs." A second time he said to him, "Simon son of John, do you love me?" He said to him, "Yes, Lord; you know that I love you." Jesus said to him, "Tend my sheep." He said to him the third time, "Simon son of John, do you love me?" Peter felt hurt because he said to him the third time, "Do you love me?" And he said to him, "Lord, you know everything; you know that I love you." Jesus said to him, "Feed my sheep."

John 21:15-17

The Church of the Primacy with the "Mensa Christi" (Christ's Table)

51

Just as Jesus began his ministry by the Sea of Galilee, so he ended it there as well. In Tabgha, on the northwestern shore of the sea, stands the Sanctuary of the Primacy of Peter. It was built by the Franciscans in 1933 on the waterfront, next to ancient steps leading down to the sea. Here, tradition holds, Jesus appeared to his disciples following the resurrection and restored Simon to his place of authority in the Church following his denials. A flat rock, known as the "Mensa Christi" or "Christ's Table," marks the site where the disciples ate that day. This rock was incorporated into the ancient churches that stood here as well as the more recent church.

Other Sites in the Northern Regions of the Holy Land

The Golan Heights

The Golan Heights rises above the Sea of Galilee and the Hula Valley. Because of its high elevation, its vantage points are numerous and breathtaking. Looking west from the hilltops, one can see the agricultural fields of the Hula Valley as an intricate and colorful patchwork. To its southwest lie the Sea of Galilee and the Jordan River, which look like the "eye" of the needle and the "thread" with which the patchwork is sown. To the east is the state of Syria. Through the years many soldiers have died or been injured in battles fought in this area. In the Golan, monuments commemorate the casualties of these hard-fought campaigns.

An ancient burial ground of "Dolmens," Gamla Nature Reserve

Natural beauty characterizes the Golan Heights. Volcanic eruptions, long since silent, have left a cover of dark volcanic rock over which flow many streams. Pockets of fertile soil along the riverbeds support dense and abundant vegetation. The plant life and plentiful water in the streams serve as a wonderful breeding ground and shelter for all kinds of wildlife. Visitors to the area find its scenery attractive and its geological formations unique.

In the center of the Golan Heights is the town of **Katzrin**. Within its city limits can be found the **Ancient Katzrin (Qusrin) Archaeological Park,** which contains the ruins of a Jewish Talmudic village. Many of the artifacts from the site are displayed in the **Golan Archaeological Museum** in Katzrin.

The antiquities site of Hammat Gader

The Hula Valley

Flock of migrant pelicans in Hula Valley

Lying between the Galilee Mountains and the Golan Heights is the Hula Valley, an area rich in water. The Jordan River courses through its center. Three streams flow into its waters: the Dan, Snir (Hatzbani) and Hermon (Banias). All three attract nature lovers and tourists to their almost magical beauty and atmosphere. Each has hiking paths along their banks which incorporate not only exquisite aquatic scenery, but also a rich variety of plants.

At the time of the formation of the modern State of Israel much of the Hula Valley was swampland. Officials decided to dry out the swamps to enable the area to become habitable and agriculturally viable. In the **Hula Nature Reserve** you can still see how this area looked before it was drained.

North of the valley, in Kibbutz Dan, one can visit **Beit Ussishkin Museum** which displays the rich variety of nat-

Near by is **Tel Dan**, the site of the ancient Canaanite town of Laish (known also as Leshem; Josh. 19:47). The tribe of Dan rebuilt it and named the city Dan. (Judg 18:29). Visitors to the archaeological site can view the remains from these periods as well as other period settlements.

Tel Hazor is one of the most significant archaeological sites in the valley. It is the site of the ancient town of Hazor, one of the largest and most important towns in the ancient Holy Land. When Joshua and the Israelites entered into the Promised Land (c. 1200 B.C.), they conquered Hazor. It was said that *"Hazor was the head of all those kingdoms"* (Josh. 11:10).

The discovery of several archaeological strata indicate numerous periods of occupation which go back to the third millennium B.C. In 732 B.C. Hazor was destroyed by the Assyrians. Some of the finds extend back to the time of King Solomon who made Hazor one of his fortress cities (1 Kings 9:15).

Tel Hazor, the artificial mound of ancient Hazor

Galilee

For other sites in and around Galilee see also "Jesus in the Northern Regions of the Holy Land" pp 12-52

The beautiful, charming landscapes of Galilee extend from the Hula Valley and the Sea of Galilee on the east to the Mediterranean Sea on the west.

Galilee has several mountain ranges with valleys tucked neatly between the peaks. The highest peak is Mount Meiron with its large evergreen nature reserve. From each mountain tourists can enjoy remarkable scenery. Both the mountains and the valleys are very fertile with different varieties of plants supporting many kinds of animals.

The resources of the area have attracted humans from earliest times. Accordingly, the imprint of these cultures is still evident today beside modern settlements. The proximity of Galilee to the Sea of Galilee and the Mediterranean Sea provide visitors the opportunity to enjoy the facilities of both beaches.

The landscape of Galilee may be divided into two distinct regions: Upper Galilee to the north and Lower Galilee to the south. Elevation proves to be the determining factor for these two territories. The change of elevation creates slightly different climactic conditions, resulting in diverse flora and fauna and also some variations in human cultures over the ages.

Right: The "Good Fence" a regulated checkpoint on the border of Israel and Lebanon, nearby Metulla

S afed (Tzfat)

Safed is one of the most significant cities in Upper Galilee. It is hidden high among the mountains as if nature conspired to keep its beauty to itself. Traces of its past appear in its many sites: a castle from the Crusader era, a mosque from the days of Muslim rule, and especially all the synagogues in its Old City, memories of the time when Safed was the spiritual center of Jewish life.

In the sixteenth century A.D., Sephardic Jews from Spain settled in Safed. The town became a great center of Jewish learning and culture. Thereafter Ashkenazi Jews were also attracted to Safed. During this "Golden Age" of the city some of the greatest Jewish scholars lived and worked here, including Rabbi Isaac Luria, who specialized in Kabbalah (the traditional term for the esoteric teachings of Judaism and for Jewish mysticism). During the eighteenth century a large number of Hasidic Jews arrived in Safed. According to some, this led to the second golden age of Safed.

Several times during its history earthquakes have severely damaged Safed. Nevertheless, the faithful return to settle here and embrace its vital past. Along with Jerusalem, Hebron and Tiberias, Safed is considered one of the four sacred Jewish cities.

Tourists can trace the steps of great Jewish scholars through the alleyways of the Old City to the synagogues and other attractions which commemorate their influence upon Judaism. One can enjoy the magical atmosphere of the Old City as its predominantly Jewish citizens keep their religious traditions alive. Guests can visit the synagogues of several different Jewish sects. All are active and hold prayer services daily. Fridays are particularly interesting as the faithful sing and pray to welcome the coming of the Sabbath.

The Artists' Quarter in the Old City contains many workshops and galleries. Every year the town celebrates the "Klezimer Festival" of Jewish music.

cco (Acre)

Acco is a port city on the Mediterranean with a special beauty and unique atmosphere that has been formed over several thousand years.

In the Old Testament this town was known as Acco, a Canaanite settlement. (Judg. 1:31). In the third century B.C. the Greeks changed the name of the city to "Ptolemais." This was the city's name when the apostle Paul stopped there on his way to Caesarea (Acts 21:7).

R osh Hanikra

Rosh Hanikra is the northernmost point of Israel on the Mediterranean coast and stands on Israel's border with Lebanon. It sits atop a limestone and chalk mountain, its western cliffs sloping to the sea. Since creation the forces of nature have carved grottos and tidal caverns into the rock. These are incredibly beautiful. Tourists gain access to the grottos via cable car.

The city's heyday occurred during the Crusades. The Crusaders made Acco their capital after having lost Jerusalem in the twelfth century. The Crusaders left a legacy of many splendid buildings. Most impressive are the enormous underground halls, known as the **knights' halls**. Originally these halls were situated above ground level and used for living quarters, official ceremonial functions and dining halls. The largest hall is the refectory of the order of St. John, built in the twelfth century.

In 1292 the Muslims destroyed Acco after the Crusades failed to liberate the Holy Land for Christians. Several hundred years later, however, the city began to thrive once again under local rulers during the Ottoman period. The city was rebuilt by the Druze Fakhr ed-Din and flourished in the eighteenth century under Dhahir el 'Amr and after him Ahmed el-Jazzar. Ahmed el-Jazzar rebuilt much of the conquered city and erected a large, attractive mosque, a Turkish bath and other buildings like "Khan el Umdan" - used as an inn and a place for trade.

In 1799 Napoleon tried to conquer the city, but he did not succeed.

The past and present blend well within this vivacious city.

Above: "Double Cross" from the Crusader Period, used for carrying relics. On display at Kibbutz Sdot-Yam Museum.   Below:Rosh Hanikra Grottos

Zippori (Sepphoris)

A Roman theater, public buildings, a Jewish residential quarter, synagogues, a colonnaded street, a church, a Crusader citadel, and an impressive water supply system--all these are only part of what has been uncovered at Zippori and its environs in Lower Galilee. Most of the remains are from the Roman and Byzantine periods, Zippori's heyday. The city served as the capital of the district of Galilee during most years of these eras. Since it lay slightly to the north-west of Nazareth, Jesus probably visited this central city. Some scholars suggest that he passed Zippori (Sepphoris) on his way from Nazareth to Capernaum.

Through much of its history, it was a Jewish city which administered political, religious, social and cultural affairs. During the second century A.D. the Jewish council known as the Sanhedrin met here. Many educated Jews made Zippori their home. One of its chief citizens was the outstanding Rabbi Judah ha-Nasi.

During the Byzantine period, a Christian community existed alongside the Jewish one. In the time of the Crusades Zippori was a city and fortress in the province of the Galilee. According to one account, the Crusaders left Zippori to engage the Muslims in a losing effort at the battle of the Horns of Hattin in A.D. 1187.

Perhaps one of the most impressive finds in Zippori is the Roman Villa. It contains a magnificent mosaic floor in pristine condition. It depicts scenes from the life of Dionysus, the mythical god of wine. The mosaic incorporates the figure of a beautiful woman, who has come to be known as the "Mona Lisa of Galilee."

Nearby stands the **Convent of the Sisters of St. Anne.** According to one tradition, Anne, the Virgin Mary's mother, and her husband Joachim lived in Zippori.

The beautiful figure of the "Mona Lisa of Galilee" at the Roman Villa, Zippori

Mount Carmel & Haifa

The beautiful Carmel Mountain rises above the Mediterranean Sea. It has thick, natural vegetation that remains green all year round and affords magical vistas of sea, mountain and plain.

Cosmetic box, late Canaanite period; Display in Reuben and Edith Hecht Museum, University of Haifa.

Haifa

Haifa, located at the juncture of the Carmel mountain range and the coastal regions, is the third largest city of Israel. It is a port city and a major industrial, commercial and service center for the north and the entire country. At the same time, as part of Mount Carmel, Haifa possesses many varieties of plants. Its beautiful landscapes and panoramic views overlook the coastline on one side and Galilee on the other. Haifa, home of museums and universities, is also a cultural and educational center.

Peak of the Carmel – Muhraqa
On the eastern peak of the Carmel range is a monastery surrounded by a national park. The view is spectacular as the Jezreel Valley unfolds below. The monastery belongs to the Carmelite order. It was here that Elijah defeated the prophets of Baal and succeeded in proving to the people that the God of Israel is the true God (1 Kings 18:17-40).

Daliyat-el Carmel and Isfiya are two special Druze villages on Mount Carmel. The Druze are a unique faith that split from Islam in the tenth century. Visitors to their villages enjoy and appreciate Druze hospitality.

Above: Stella Maris Carmelite Monastery and Church. From the church, one can follow steps which lead down to Elijah's Cave.
Left: The Baha'i World Center Shrine and Gardens on the slope of Mount Carmel.

The Northern Valleys
Jordan Valley and Jezreel Valley

The Jordan Valley is a strip of land stretching along the banks of the Jordan River. It extends from the Sea of Galilee in the north to the Dead Sea in the south. The low-lying valley reveals part of the Syrian-African Rift, one of the most impressive geological structures in the world. In part the valley also marks Israel's border with Jordan.

This area has contributed more than any other area in the country to what is known of the Neolithic and Chalcolithic periods (8000-3300 B.C.). According to archaeological excavations in several sites, this range marked the stage between the beginning of the agricultural revolution and the establishment of the first village communities. Two key sites in the valley for this period are Jericho and Tuleilat el-Ghassul in the vicinity of the Dead Sea.

From ancient times the **Jezreel Valley** (also known as the Plain of Esdraelon) was known for its well-watered and fertile fields. The main road that linked Egypt with Mesopotamia ran through this valley. Tribal leaders and outside aggressors coveted the valley for its location and abundance. Frequent battles in the region often determined who ruled this part of the Holy Land.

Its importance is indicated by its frequent appearances in the Old Testament. The prophet Hosea remarks: *"And the earth shall answer the grain, the wine, and the oil, and they shall answer Jezreel"* (Hos. 2:22).

South of the Valley of Jezreel stands majestic **Mount Gilboa.** On this mountain King Saul died by his own sword while fighting against the Philistines (1 Sam. 31). Afterwards David lamented the death of the king and his dear friend jonathan, the King's son (2 Samuel 1:19-21).

Left: The Crusader fortress of "Belvoir", established as a fortified farm, rests on the crest of the heights above the Jordan Valley. Below: Jezreel Valley

B eth Shean

The discoveries made in Beth Shean, one of the oldest cities in the Holy Land, demonstrate the long and glorious history of the town. The finds extend over a large area and include: a theater, an amphitheater, an enormous bath-house, wide streets adorned with columns, massive public buildings, a basilica and many other antiquities. At earlier levels, from the sixteenth to the twelfth centuries B.C., the artificial mound of Beth Shean (Tel Beth Shean) yielded finds from the Egyptian reigns of Thutmose III, Seti I and Ramses II. Further excavations at the tel reveal more remains from the Canaanite and Israelite settlements.

The importance of the town since ancient times has resulted from its location at a major crossroads. In addition the surrounding land is fertile and water is in abundance.

Biblical "Beth Shan" may be best known for the horrific story in which the city following the battle at Gilboa (1 Sam. 31:8-13). King Solomon recognized the value of the area and set one of his officers over the region (1 Kings 4:12). From the Hellenistic period the city was called "Scythopolis" and "Nysa" after the nursemaid of Dionysus, the mythical god of wine.

The city reached the height of its prosperity during the Roman and Byzantine periods. During the sixth century A.D. it may have had as many as forty thousand residents. At the end of the Byzantine period the city fell under Muslim control and was later devastated by an earthquake in A.D. 749. In more modern times the city, as in the ancient past, serves as a regional center for the surrounding countryside, which is mainly agricultural.

Ancient jar in the Museum of Regional and Mediterranean Archaeology, Gan Hashlosha.

M egiddo (Armageddon)

Megiddo lies on the western edge of the Jezreel Valley. Because of its location it controlled the main routes passing through the region in earlier times. Archaeologists have uncovered more than twenty different layers of occupation at Tel Megiddo, the mound of ancient Megiddo. These provide some knowledge of all the peoples who occupied the site over several thousand years. "Armageddon" is a corrupt spelling of the Hebrew "Har-megiddo" which means "mountain of Megiddo."

Many an ancient conqueror has marched on the routes leading to Megiddo. Throughout history many armies did battle there. The Egyptian Thutmose III turned Megiddo into a major Egyptian base in the fifteenth century B.C. During the period of the Judges Megiddo was one of the Canaanite cities in the valley (Judg. 5:19). Later it fell into Israelite hands and King Solomon made it one of his chief administrative districts (1 Kings 4:12).

According to the book of Revelation, the kings of the earth will gather here for the final battle between good and evil (Rev. 16:12-16).

Above: Subterranean water system, 9th century B.C., Megiddo
Below: Archaeological mound of Megiddo

Caesarea

Caesarea is one of the most magnificent and interesting archaeological sites on the coast of the Holy Land. In the first century B.C. Herod the Great rebuilt the town over a settlement called "Straton's Tower." He named it "Caesarea" in honor of the Roman Emperor Augustus.

Planned and built according to exacting standards, Caesarea's walls encompassed a temple, a royal palace, a theater, an amphitheater, a hippodrome, a market area, homes and public buildings. Its Herodian port was actually an artificial harbor which took twelve years to construct. When the Romans annexed Judea to the empire in A.D. 6, they made Caesarea the headquarters of the provincial governor and his administration. One of the special finds at Caesarea contains an inscription referring to Pontius Pilate, the Procurator (governor) of Judea in A.D. 26-36.

Caesarea figures prominently in many events recorded in the Acts of the Apostles. (Including Acts 8:40, Acts 23:23-33, and Acts 24:27-26:32). Perhaps the most significant event occurred here when Simon Peter shared the gospel with Cornelius, a Roman centurion who became the first Gentile convert (Acts 10:44-48).

During the Roman and Byzantine periods Caesarea continued to flourish and expand. In the third century A.D. a center for the study of Christian theology, philosophy and religion was established in Caesarea by Origen of Alexandria. The school housed one of the most important Christian libraries in the East. Eusebius, an early church writer and theologian, became bishop of Caesarea in the fourth century. Alongside the Christian community, a Jewish community with Jewish scholars continued to thrive.

When Arabs conquered the area in the seventh century A.D., Caesarea continued to exist but it lost its political and economic standing. However, during the Crusades, the city was fortified with a massive wall and moat. Many splendid archaeological sites continue to teach us about Caesarea's past.

*Left: A Roman statue on display at **The Museum of Caesarea Antiquities** at nearby Kibbutz Sdot-Yam.   Below: Caesarea's large theater*

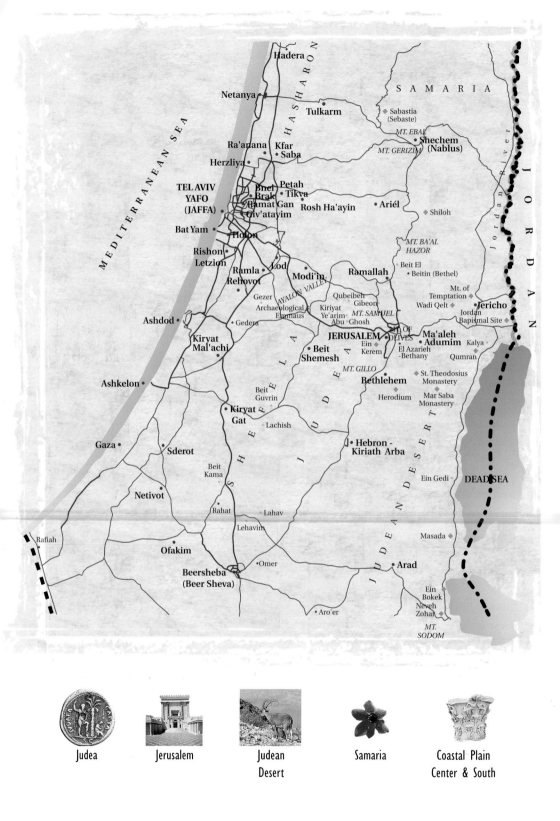

MEDITERRANEAN SEA

Hadera
Netanya
HASHARON
Tulkarm
Sabastia (Sebaste)
S A M A R I A

Ra'anana
Kfar Saba
MT. EBAL
Shechem (Nablus)
MT. GERIZIM

Herzliya

TEL AVIV YAFO (JAFFA)
Bnei Brak
Petah Tikva
Ariél
Shiloh
Ramat Gan
Giv'atayim
Rosh Ha'ayin

Bat Yam
Holon

MT. BA'AL HAZOR

Rishon Letzion
Ramla
Lod
Modi'in
Ramallah
Beit El
Beitin (Bethel)
Rehovot

Gezer
Archaeological Emmaus
AYALON VALLEY
Qubeibeh
Gibeon
Wadi Qelt
Mt. of Temptation
Jericho

Ashdod
Gedera
Kiryat Ye'arim
Abu Ghosh
MT. SAMUEL
Jordan Bapismal Site

Kiryat Mal'achi
JERUSALEM
MT. OF OLIVES
Ma'aleh Adumim
Kalya

Ashkelon
Ein Kerem
El Azarieh -Bethany
Qumran

Beit Shemesh

MT. GILLO
Bethlehem
St. Theodosius Monastery

Beit Guvrin
Herodium
Mar Saba Monastery

Gaza
Kiryat Gat
Lachish

Sderot
Hebron - Kiriath Arba

Beit Kama
Ein Gedi
DEAD SEA

Netivot
Rahat
Lahav

Lehavim
Masada

Rafiah
Ofakim

Omer
Arad

Beersheba (Beer Sheva)
Ein Bokek
Neveh Zohar

Aro'er
MT. SODOM

J U D E A
S H E F E L A
J U D E A N   D E S E R T
JORDAN
Jordan River

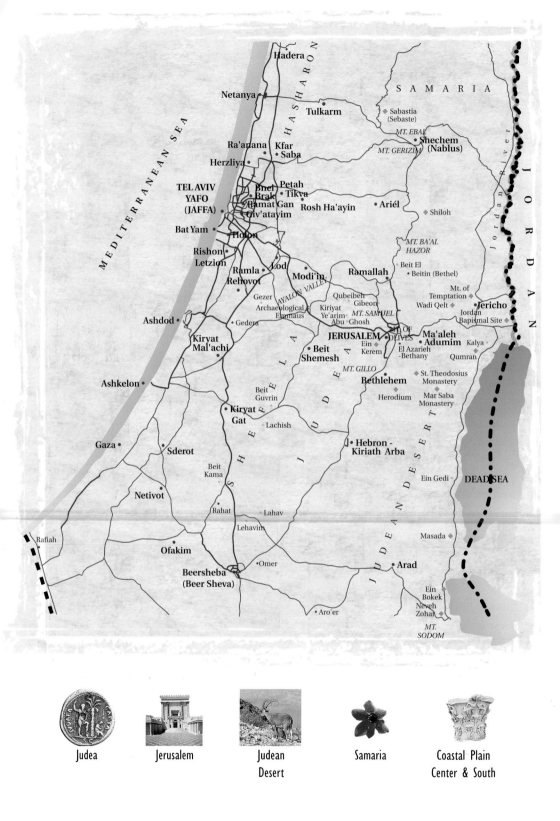

Judea   Jerusalem   Judean Desert   Samaria   Coastal Plain Center & South

In the wake of the peace process, certain areas of Judea, Samaria and the Gaza Strip have been transferred, or are in the process of being transferred, to the Palestinian Jurisdiction.

Jesus
in the Central Regions
of the Holy Land

The central regions of the Holy Land include some of the most important sites in the country.

At the heart of the Holy Land is Jerusalem, the city of peace, the holy city of the Prophets. It is a city sacred to the world's major monotheistic religions. Here, the infant Jesus was presented at the temple by his parents, and here, in his final days, he walked his last steps. Outside the city gates he was crucified. Guests to Jerusalem can step on the same stones upon which these events occurred and feel in the air that the "stones speak for themselves."

South of Jerusalem lies Bethlehem, the birthplace of Jesus, the hometown of David. In its vicinity are situated the shepherds' fields where an angel appeared and told the young men about the birth of the Savior.

The Judean mountains encircle Jerusalem, which rises majestically from their center. North of Judea lies the area of Samaria. East of Judea, the Judean Desert drifts down to the lowest point on the face of the earth, the Dead Sea.

West of Jerusalem the highlands become fertile plains and the plains become the white sands that run along the Mediterranean coast. Situated in the middle of the shoreline is the city of Tel Aviv-Jaffa (Yaffo), the country's major economic and cultural center.

The importance of these sites does not hide the outstanding scenery with its magnificent beauty. Moreover, the central regions are rich in archaeological significance and the ruins of past civilizations that witnessed history's dramatic events. Recently they have begun to reveal their secrets kept for thousands of years.

E in Kerem (Ein Karem)

When the angel Gabriel appeared to Mary in Nazareth, he informed her not only of her own role in God's plan, but he also said to her:

> *"And now, your relative Elizabeth in her old age has also conceived a son; and this is the sixth month for her who was said to be barren. For nothing will be impossible with God."*
>
> Luke 1:36-37

Today, Ein Kerem, located in Judea, is part of western Jerusalem. It was the home of Elizabeth and Zechariah, the parents of John the Baptist. One day, as Zechariah was serving as priest in the temple, the angel Gabriel appeared to him and told him that he would have a son who would go forth in the spirit and power of Elijah. He would ready the people for the coming of the Lord (Luke 1:5-20).

Tablets in the Church of the Visitation courtyard feature excerpts from Mary's "Magnificat" in several languages.

During the sixth month of Elizabeth's pregnancy, Mary visited her in Judea. As she heard Mary's greeting, the child within her leaped in the womb. Mary exclaimed praise to God for his magnificent blessings--a text referred to as the "Magnificat" in church tradition:

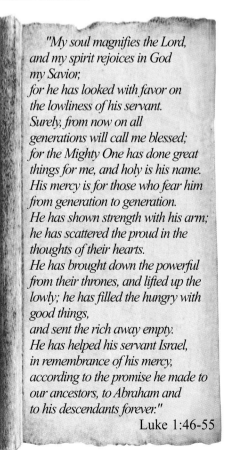

> *"My soul magnifies the Lord, and my spirit rejoices in God my Savior;*
> *for he has looked with favor on the lowliness of his servant.*
> *Surely, from now on all generations will call me blessed;*
> *for the Mighty One has done great things for me, and holy is his name.*
> *His mercy is for those who fear him from generation to generation.*
> *He has shown strength with his arm; he has scattered the proud in the thoughts of their hearts.*
> *He has brought down the powerful from their thrones, and lifted up the lowly; he has filled the hungry with good things,*
> *and sent the rich away empty.*
> *He has helped his servant Israel, in remembrance of his mercy,*
> *according to the promise he made to our ancestors, to Abraham and to his descendants forever."*
>
> Luke 1:46-55

Opposite page: The steeple of the Church of St. John adorns the skyline of Ein Kerem.

The Church of St. John

After Elizabeth gave birth to her son, they circumcised him on the eighth day and gave him the name "John" (Luke 1:57-66).

Nestled between the hills around Jerusalem, modern Ein Kerem is a charming neighborhood of Jerusalem blessed with a pastoral atmosphere. In the center of the village sits the well, where, according to tradition, Mary met Elizabeth. The houses of the village are made of stone. Scattered among the houses, church steeples adorn the skyline of Ein Kerem.

There are several churches and monasteries in and around Ein Kerem:

The Church of St. John, a Franciscan church, was built over the sacred spot where John the Baptist was born. The church courtyard displays tablets, inscribed in several languages, on which the prophecy of Zechariah is written. He uttered this prophecy on the day they came to circumcise and name John (Luke 1:67-79), referred to as the "Benedictus" in church tradition.

The Church of the Visitation, a Franciscan church, honors the occasion of the Virgin Mary's visit.

A beautiful mosaic depicting Mary on her journey from Nazareth to Jerusalem decorates the exterior of the church. Tablets in the church courtyard record Mary's "Magnificat" (Luke 1:46-55) in several languages.

Exterior mosaic on the Church of the Visitation

There are also a number of active monastic communities in modern Ein Kerem. These include the Monastery of John the Baptist, the Russian Orthodox church and Convent and the Convent of "Notre Dame de Sion" with its beautiful hostel.

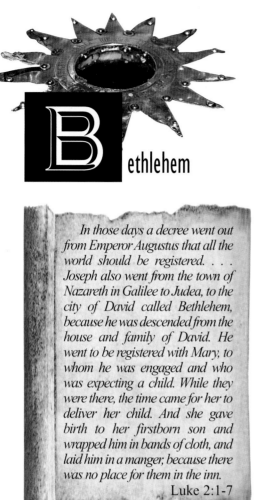

Bethlehem

> In those days a decree went out from Emperor Augustus that all the world should be registered. . . . Joseph also went from the town of Nazareth in Galilee to Judea, to the city of David called Bethlehem, because he was descended from the house and family of David. He went to be registered with Mary, to whom he was engaged and who was expecting a child. While they were there, the time came for her to deliver her child. And she gave birth to her firstborn son and wrapped him in bands of cloth, and laid him in a manger, because there was no place for them in the inn.
>
> Luke 2:1-7

Exterior of the Church of the Nativity

Bethlehem, the birthplace of Jesus, lies to the south of Jerusalem. It has its own special character and is of great historic importance. It is the hometown of David. Here, Samuel anointed David to be King of Israel (1 Sam. 16:1-13). According to the prophet Micah, one day God would raise up a ruler to lead the people of Israel from Bethlehem:

But you, O Bethlehem of Ephrathah,
who are one of the little clans of Judah,
from you shall come forth for me one who is to rule in Israel,
whose origin is from of old, from ancient days.

Micah 5:2

Rachel, Jacob's wife and one of the four matriarchs of Israel, is buried in the territory of Bethlehem (Gen. 35:19). The story of Ruth the Moabite, the great grandmother of King David, unfolds in the fields around the town (Ruth 1-4). Clearly Bethlehem ranks as a significant site for the stories of the Old Testament.

Bethlehem is located on the mountain road which, from ancient times, linked the main hilltop cities of Samaria, Shechem, Bethel, Jerusalem, Bethlehem and Hebron on a north-south route. Near Bethlehem a major route crossed east to west, leading down to the desert. Bethlehem's location at the edge of the desert made it a meeting place for farmers, shepherds and the nomadic peoples of the desert.

In Hebrew "Bethlehem" means "House of Bread." In Arabic it means "House of Meat."

The rural setting gives Bethlehem a special, pastoral atmosphere. Church steeples, visible from far distances, add to the city's charm and act as a constant reminder of the many important events that occurred in this area. A visit to Bethlehem always induces an exhilarating and uplifting feeling.

The Basilica of the Nativity

Opposite page: An ariel view of Bethlehem with the Church of the Nativity in the center

The "Star of Bethlehem"
in the Grotto of the Nativity

The Church of the Nativity

The Church of the Nativity was built above the **Grotto of the Nativity** in which Jesus was born. In the eastern side of the grotto is a circular recess, containing a large silver star which designates the spot where, as tradition has it, Jesus was born. The star has fourteen points and is inscribed with a Latin inscription which translates: "HERE JESUS CHRIST WAS BORN OF THE VIRGIN MARY."

Above the star is a remnant of a Crusader mosaic depicting the revelation of the birth. Next to the circular recess is the **Holy Manger**. The manger is hewn out of stone and covered with marble strips. Next to it is an altar devoted to the Three Wise Men who saw the star in the east and came to worship the baby Jesus.

The Holy Manger in the Grotto of the Nativity

Opposite page: Christmas procession in Bethlehem

And she gave birth to her firstborn son and wrapped him in bands of cloth, and laid him in a manger, because there was no place for them in the inn.

Luke 2:7

In the time of King Herod, after Jesus was born in Bethlehem of Judea, wise men from the East came to Jerusalem, asking, "Where is the child who has been born king of the Jews? For we observed his star at its rising, and have come to pay him homage." When King Herod heard this, he was frightened, and all Jerusalem with him; ... Then he sent them to Bethlehem, ... When they had heard the king, they set out; and there, ahead of them, went the star that they had seen at its rising, until it stopped over the place where the child was. When they saw that the star had stopped, they were overwhelmed with joy. On entering the house, they saw the child with Mary his mother; and they knelt down and paid him homage. Then, opening their treasure chests, they offered him gifts of gold, frankincense, and myrrh.

Matthew 2:1-11

The Basilica of St. Catherine

The first church was built above the Grotto of the Nativity in the fourth century A.D. by the Roman Emperor Constantine. Through his edict he proclaimed Christianity a legal religion in the Roman Empire and thereby sanctioned Christian worship. Constantine and his mother, Helena, built a majestic church adorned with mosaics, frescoes and beautiful marble.

In the sixth century the Byzantine Emperor Justinian built a new and even more elaborate church here. Its walls, as well as those of the grotto and the entrance to it, were covered with marble and gold-plated mosaics. During the seventh century, when the Persians invaded the Holy Land, they destroyed all Christian churches they found except for the Church of

the Nativity. According to one legend, when the Persians saw the mosaics depicting the wise men from the east coming to pay homage to Jesus (Matt. 2:9-11), they were astonished by the sight of the Persian sages. Out of respect for them, they left the church intact.

In the eleventh century, the Crusaders hoisted their flag above the basilica. The church was renovated and many pilgrims came to worship there. The Crusader King Baldwin I chose to be crowned here on Christmas Day in 1101.

After the Crusader era, the church suffered destruction and pillage. However, as if by a miracle, despite all the conflicts waged in the area, the church remained intact on its foundations.

An altar in the lower level of the Church of the Nativity

The church building which stands today is essentially the same as the one erected during the time of Justinian, with the additions of the Crusaders. Some of the best artists of these eras contributed to the masterful blend of mosaics and paintings which adorned the floors, columns and walls of this magnificent structure.

The church is cared for by the Greek Orthodox, Armenian Orthodox and Franciscan Catholics.

Next to the basilica constructed by Justinian stands the **Basilica of St. Catherine** (Franciscan) built on the foundations of a Crusader Church erected in the twelfth century.

The Church was dedicated to Saint Catherine, who died as a martyr in Egypt during the fourth century. The chapel to the right of the Basilica is dedicated to Jesus' birth. A statue of the baby Jesus sits under the altar.

Located outside Saint Catherine's Basilica is the Cloister of St. Jerome (Hieronymus). St. Jerome is perhaps best known for translating the Bible into Latin. His translation is called the Vulgate. In the fourth century he began a monastery in Bethlehem and lived there.

On the lower level of the church are underground coves which house the Chapel of the Innocents (Matt. 2:16-18), the Chapel of St. Joseph (Matt. 2:13-15), and St. Jerome's Room. There are also tombs which commemorate the burial site of St. Jerome and several of his co-workers.

Interior of the Basilica of the Nativity

During Christmas celebrations, the traditional Mass Parade begins at St. Catherine's Basilica and travels toward the Grotto of the Nativity. The parade is broadcast worldwide on television and radio.

The image of the baby Jesus in the Basilica of St. Catherine is removed for Christmas and placed in the Holy Manger.

Other important churches and monasteries are found in the region of Bethlehem. **The Milk Grotto** (Franciscan) hallows the ground where, as tradition has it, Mary hid before her escape to Egypt. While feeding the infant Jesus, a drop of her milk is purported to have dropped to the floor. The grotto is hewn from white rock and lavishly decorated.

The Ancient Church of Mary's Rock
Kathisma Church

In 1992 authorities uncovered the remains of a large, octagonal church built in the Byzantine period. At the heart of the structure was found a large, flat rock elevated above the surrounding floor. According to tradition, the pregnant Mary rested on this stone during her difficult journey from Nazareth to Bethlehem. It is probably one of the earliest churches dedicated to the Virgin Mother of Christ.

The archaeological discoveries from the 5th century church north of Bethlehem, including Mary's Rock

Figurine depicting a pregnant woman 6th-5th centuries B.C. (Display in Reuben and Edith Hecht Museum, University of Haifa.)

Rachel's Tomb

Rachel, Jacob's wife and one of the four matriarchs of Israel, is buried in the territory of Bethlehem.

The traditional tomb is located on the main mountain route *"on the way to Ephrath (that is, Bethlehem), and Jacob set up a pillar at her grave; it is the pillar of Rachel's tomb, which is there to this day"* (Gen. 35:19-20).

Matthew saw in Rachel's sorrow for her children the agony of many mothers during Herod's slaughter of the innocents.

Then was fulfilled what had been spoken through the prophet Jeremiah:
"A voice was heard in Ramah, wailing and loud lamentation, Rachel weeping for her children; she refused to be consoled, because they are no more."
Matthew 2:17-18

קבר רחל אמנו

The Shepherds' Fields

The traditional Shepherds' Fields are east of Bethlehem in an area which supported the agricultural needs of Judea. The area was perfect for grazing livestock. The agricultural lands spread out as far as the Judean Desert, and those areas not used for agriculture were taken up by pasture.

The place is associated with the "tower for the flock" and is mentioned in the Old Testament (Mic. 4:8). The prophet Micah also wrote about a ruler who would one day arise from Bethlehem (Mic. 5:2). In these fields the angel alerted the shepherds that a Savior was born in Bethlehem.

There are several churches in the area built above caves considered sacred. The Franciscan's Church of the Shepherds and the Greek Orthodox church are situated near the Arab village of Beit Sahur, east of Bethlehem. The modern churches, along with the ruins of ancient churches and monasteries, continue to recall the revelation to the shepherds.

Inset lower right:
Interior of the Franciscan Church
of the Shepherds' Fields

In that region there were shepherds living in the fields, keeping watch over their flock by night. Then an angel of the Lord stood before them, and the glory of the Lord shone around them, and they were terrified. But the angel said to them, "Do not be afraid; for see— I am bringing you good news of great joy for all the people: to you is born this day in the city of David a Savior, who is the Messiah, the Lord. This will be a sign for you: you will find a child wrapped in bands of cloth and lying in a manger." And suddenly there was with the angel a multitude of the heavenly host, praising God and saying, "Glory to God in the highest heaven, and on earth peace among those whom he favors!" …

So they went with haste and found Mary and Joseph, and the child lying in the manger. When they saw this, they made known what had been told them about this child; and all who heard it were amazed at what the shepherds told them.

Luke 2:8-18

"The Baptism of Jesus by John"
The painting is located in the Church of St. John in Ein Kerem.

Baptism of Jesus

In those days John the Baptist appeared in the wilderness of Judea, proclaiming, "Repent, for the kingdom of heaven has come near." This is the one of whom the prophet Isaiah spoke when he said,

"The voice of one crying out in the wilderness:
'Prepare the way of the Lord, make his paths straight.'"

Matthew 3:1-3

In those days Jesus came from Nazareth of Galilee and was baptized by John in the Jordan. And just as he was coming up out of the water, he saw the heavens torn apart and the Spirit descending like a dove on him. And a voice came from heaven, "You are my Son, the Beloved; with you I am well pleased."

Mark 1:9-11

The Jordan River flows south from the Sea of Galilee through the Syrian-African Rift to the Dead Sea. Many prophets in Israel found inspiration and comfort in the area around the Jordan. Elijah hid by the Wadi Cherith after he confronted Ahab with the word of the Lord (1 Kings 17:3). Elisha sent Naaman, the commander of the army for the king of Aram, to the Jordan and told him to wash seven times so his leprosy would be cured (2 Kings 5:8-14).

John the Baptist chose the Jordan to prepare the way for the Lord's coming. In these waters he baptized Jesus of Nazareth, an event which marked the beginning of the Savior's public ministry.

Nearby, more than one-thousand-two-hundred years earlier, the Israelites had crossed the Jordan and entered the Promised Land (Joshua 3).

Located on the banks of the Jordan River in the area east of Jericho, a number of churches and monasteries celebrate the place where John baptized Jesus and preached to the crowd, and where the Israelites entered into the Holy Land.

Greek Orthodox procession near the location of the Baptism in the lower Jordan River

Mount of Temptation

Then Jesus was led up by the Spirit into the wilderness to be tempted by the devil. He fasted forty days and forty nights, and afterwards he was famished. The tempter came and said to him,"If you are the Son of God, command these stones to become loaves of bread." But he answered, "It is written,

'One does not live by bread alone, but by every word that comes from the mouth of God.'"

Matthew 4:1-4

Again, the devil took him to a very high mountain and showed him all the kingdoms of the world and their splendor; and he said to him, "All these I will give you, if you will fall down and worship me." Jesus said to him, "Away with you, Satan! for it is written,

'Worship the Lord your God, and serve only him.'"

Then the devil left him, and suddenly angels came and waited on him.

Matthew 4:8-11

The Mount of Temptation, according to tradition, stands northwest of Jericho, overlooking the world's most ancient city. According to the New Testament, it was here that the devil tried to tempt Jesus after his baptism by John in the Jordan River. Jesus had withdrawn to the desert to fast and reflect on his destiny. When forty days of fasting were over, the devil came to him, enticing him to turn rocks into bread. Jesus refused to submit to the devil's temptation. The summit of the mountain represents the place where the devil showed Jesus all the kingdoms of the world and demanded his worship.

On the mountain's face are many caves which monks from the fourth century A.D. on used as places of solitude. In the years that followed, several monasteries were built nearby. Today, on the slope of the mount stands the **Greek Orthodox Temptation Monastery** known also as the **"Quarantal Monastery"** (a corruption of the word "quarante," meaning "forty"). It is particularly outstanding because its designers utilized the cliff face as part of the structure. From its balcony visitors enjoy a scenic view of Jericho and the Jordan Valley.

The Greek Orthodox Temptation Monastery

The Area of Samaria

Samaria refers to the area north of Judea that contains the central hill country of the Holy Land. In the time of Jesus this area was inhabited by the Samaritans.

In the eighth century B.C. Israel fell to the Assyrians and some of its inhabitants were deported. Following the exile, the Kings of Assyria brought people from *"Babylon, Cuthah, Avva, Hamath, and Sepharvaim, and placed them in the cities of Samaria* (2 Kings 17:24). They mixed with the local Israelite population, creating an increasing cultural and religious amalgamation. Nevertheless, in the course of time, a Samaritan community arose in Samaria.

The Gospel of Luke records that Jesus encountered ten lepers in a village at the border of Samaria and Galilee. They cried out to him for mercy and he healed them. One returned, a Samaritan, to thank Jesus for this precious gift (Luke 17:11-19).

The Samaritans are today a small ethnic group. They consider themselves to be descended from the Israelites. They believe only in the first five books of Moses and practice only those rites mentioned in the Torah. Mount Gerizim is their spiritual and religious center. The area of Samaria continues to serve as their residential center, and their second is in Holon, south of Tel Aviv.

Ruins from the ancient city of Sebaste

Samaria (Sebaste)

In the time of the Old Testament, Omri, king of Israel, purchased a hill from a man named Shemer and built a city there which he named Samaria after its former owner (1 Kings 16:24). Samaria was the capital city of the Kingdom of Israel and has continued to be an important administrative center for the region. In 333 B.C. when the Persian empire fell to Alexander the Great, Samaria too was conquered, and Macedonian soldiers were settled here, turning it into a purely pagan city. During the period of Roman rule, King Herod built here the magnificent city of Sebaste to honor Caesar Augustus.

One tradition holds that John the Baptist was buried in the territory of Samaria, although other stories give a different account. The historian Josephus indicates that Herod Antipas imprisoned John at Machaerus, on the eastern side of the Dead Sea (*Antiquities* 18.5.2). John had criticized him for an unlawful marriage to his brother's wife, Herodias. After her daughter danced at his birthday party, Herod foolishly promised her anything she asked for. Prompted by Herodias, the daughter asked for John's head on a platter. Though Herod did not want to kill John, he did so because his guests had witnessed his promise. John's disciples took and buried his body but scripture does not say where (Matt. 14:1-12).

According to the New Testament, Philip, Peter and John all came to preach in this city (Acts 8:5, 25).

> *Now those who were scattered went from place to place, proclaiming the word. Philip went down to the city of Samaria and proclaimed the Messiah to them. The crowds with one accord listened eagerly to what was said by Philip, hearing and seeing the signs that he did, for unclean spirits, crying with loud shrieks, came out of many who were possessed; and many others who were paralyzed or lame were cured. So there was great joy in that city.*
>
> Acts 8:4-8

The old city of Sebaste contains the remains of Byzantine and Crusader churches dedicated to John the Baptist. During the Crusader period the city was rebuilt with a cathedral dedicated to John the Baptist. Today, the site is identified with the Arab village of "Sabastia" which continues to carry the old Roman name.

Jacob's Well

Shechem (Nablus)

The city of Shechem lies between Mount Gerizim and Mount Ebal in a fertile valley which has attracted settlers throughout history. It is first mentioned in the Old Testament when Abram and Jacob passed through the territory and built altars there. After the division of Israel, Jeroboam built Shechem and resided there (1 Kings 12:25). The Arabic name of the city today, Nablus, is a corruption of the Greek "Neapolis" – the name given to Shechem in the Hellenistic period. Tel Balatah, east of the modern city, is the site of the Old Testament and the Hellenistic village. Archaeological excavations unearthed a wealth of finds from as early as the Chalcolithic period.

The Oak of Moreh stands near Shechem and recalls God's appearance to Abram and the divine promise to give his ancestors the land. Abram built an altar to the Lord near the sacred tree of Moreh (Gen. 12:5-7). After many years Jacob purchased a tract of land at Shechem and built an altar there which he called "El-Elohe-Israel" ("God, the God of Israel"; Gen. 33:18-20). After Joseph died, the Israelites brought his bones back from Egypt and buried them in that same field (Josh. 24:32).

Jacob's Well

The well is situated on the land that Jacob purchased at Shechem. It is also the important site where Jesus met the Samaritan woman and asked her for a drink of water (John 4:1-42).

He left Judea and started back to Galilee. But he had to go through Samaria. So he came to a Samaritan city called Sychar, near the plot of ground that Jacob had given to his son Joseph. Jacob's well was there, and Jesus, tired out by his journey, was sitting by the well. It was about noon.

A Samaritan woman came to draw water, and Jesus said to her, "Give me a drink."... The Samaritan woman said to him, "How is it that you, a Jew, ask a drink of me, a woman of Samaria?"... Jesus answered her, "If you knew the gift of God, and who it is that is saying to you, 'Give me a drink,' you would have asked him, and he would have given you living water."

The waving of the Torah Scrolls during the Samaritan's ceremony of Mount Gerizim

Mount Gerizim

Mount Gerizim and Mount Ebal mark the highest points of elevation in the region. After the Israelites crossed the Jordan, they erected an altar on Mount Ebal and set up stones inscribed with the words of the Law (Josh. 8:30ff.). Mount Ebal became known as the Mount of Cursing because Moses commanded certain tribes to gather atop Ebal as the Levites pronounced curses on all who broke God's Law (Deut. 27:11-26). Moses ordered certain tribes to assemble on Gerizim's summit to represent God's blessing on the faithful and obedient (Deut. 27:11).

Mount Gerizim, according to the Samaritans' doctrine, is the site where Abraham erected an altar to sacrifice his son, Isaac (Gen. 22:1-19). Every year they celebrate Passover Eve by sacrificing lambs on Mount Gerizim.

The woman said to him, "Sir, you have no bucket, and the well is deep. Where do you get that living water? Are you greater than our ancestor Jacob, who gave us the well, and with his sons and his flocks drank from it?" Jesus said to her, "Everyone who drinks of this water will be thirsty again, but those who drink of the water that I will give them will never be thirsty. The water that I will give will become in them a spring of water gushing up to eternal life."... The woman said to him, "I know that Messiah is coming" (who is called Christ). "When he comes, he will proclaim all things to us." Jesus said to her, "I am he, the one who is speaking to you."

John 4:3-26

87

J ericho

On his final journey to Jerusalem Jesus passed through Jericho. While in Jericho, Jesus met Zacchaeus, the chief tax collector in the region. The publican climbed a tree to get a better look as the Lord was passing through. Jesus saw him, called him down from the tree and went home with him that day. Later, because of his encounter with Jesus, he decided to dedicate half his wealth to the poor and promised to make restitution to all whom he had defrauded (Luke 19:1-10).

Perhaps no desert oasis is more stunning than Jericho. Its natural springs have provided supplies for all its inhabitants through many millennia. In addition its location on the main route along the Jordan River and up to the western mountains, made Jericho one of the oldest cities in the world, continuously inhabited over the last ten thousand years. The vegetation which blankets the city appears to give a green glow to the desert and its surroundings.

The Old Testament mentions Jericho many times. Nearby the Israelites crossed the Jordan River on their way to the Promised Land (Joshua 3:14-16).

Jericho was the first city conquered by Joshua and the Israelites after crossing the Jordan. Led by the priests who carried the ark of the Lord, they marched around the city one time per day for six days. On the seventh day they marched around the city seven times, the priests blew their trumpets, the people shouted and the wall protecting the city fell (Josh. 6:12-21).

Tel Jericho, the artificial mound of ancient Jericho

During the Hellenistic-Roman period, especially in the time of the Hasmoneans and King Herod, Jericho reached its pinnacle of prosperity. Ancient engineers diverted water to this populous city from nearby springs and streams. More and more land was taken up into gardens and agricultural lands. In the favorable climate of this area the groves of Jericho produced high quality dates and various medicinal plants and spices, particularly balsam. Because of its favorable winter climate Jericho also became a prestigious spot to build luxurious palaces and summer homes.

During the Byzantine period Jericho and its vicinity became an important Christian haven with many churches and monasteries built there. There were also some synagogues erected there in the Byzantine period as well. These indicate that the settlement included a Jewish community. Muslims began settling in Jericho during the seventh and eighth centuries. The Umayyad rulers built one of their splendid winter palaces near Jericho.

Tel Jericho (Tell es-Sultan), the artificial mound of ancient Jericho, has revealed layers of cities and human habitation reaching back more then ten thousand years. The finds in these layers have earned Jericho the title "the world's oldest city."

Nearby is the large spring of ancient Jericho called in Arabic "Ein es-Sultan." The spring, also called "Elisha's Well," commemorates the Old Testament story of the miracle performed by the prophet Elisha when he sweetened the water of the spring by casting salt into it (2 King 2:19-22).

The large and impressive **Winter Palaces** dated from the time of the Hasmoneans and Herod the Great. Archaeologists uncovered towers, large halls, decorative gardens, "Mikveh", large buildings, Roman baths and swimming pools.

Ancient Jewish Synagogues include one decorated by a magnificent mosaic floor from the Byzantine era with a Hebrew inscription which reads "Shalom Al Y'israel" - "Peace upon Israel."

Hisham's Palace an eighth century Umayyed-Muslim palace with a mosque and an enormous bathhouse. Including statues, a courtyard with pillars, domed roofs, and multicolored mosaic floors.

Stone relief in Hisham's Palace

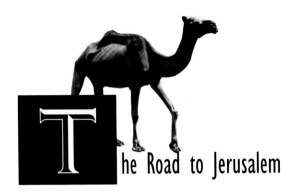

The Road to Jerusalem

On his last journey from Jericho to Jerusalem, Jesus traveled an important road, an east-to-west passage steadily ascending the mount to the Holy City. The route was full of twists and turns; robbers often hid in the shadows making the journey hazardous for many travelers. Wayside inns and fortresses were set up along the way; their remains are still evident today.

The Monastery of St. George, Wadi Qelt

The Inn of the Good Samaritan commemorates one of Jesus' most famous parables, the parable of the Good Samaritan. He told this story in reply to a lawyer's question: *"And who is my neighbor?"* (Luke 10:29).

Wadi Qelt (Nahal Parat) is one of the most beautiful and interesting streams in the country. It collects waters from the Judean countryside and runs into the Jordan near Jericho. Due to its springs a rich variety of vegetation and wildlife have evolved around the wadi. The abundant supply of water and natural caves along this route made this wadi a popular crossing between Jericho and Jerusalem. Along the edge of the wadi a Roman road led up to the Mount of Olives.

Along the stream there are remains of aqueducts, fortresses, palaces and monasteries from different periods. The most stunning of these is the **Greek Orthodox Monastery of St. George**. It was built on a sheer cliff-face overlooking the stream. According to one tradition, this is where Elijah the Prophet hid and where the ravens brought him bread and meat (1 Kings 17:2-7). Another tradition connects the place with Anne and Joachim, the mother and father of the Virgin Mary.

Bethany and Bethphage

Bethany and Bethphage are situated outside of Jerusalem on the eastern slopes of the Mount of Olives. From Bethphage a path led further down to Bethany less than two miles from Jerusalem on the road leading to Jericho. Today near the site is the Arab village of El Azarieh (of Lazarus). According to written documents and archaeological evidence, this area was settled in ancient times.

Bethany is particularly known as the place where Jesus raised Lazarus from the dead (John 11). The tomb would have been hewn in the rock within a cave with steps leading down to the burial chamber. Today in the middle of the village one can see the traditional site of the tomb. The old entrance is still visible, but is now walled up, as it forms the wall of a mosque.

In addition to Mary, Martha and Lazarus, Jesus had other friends in Bethany including Simon the leper in whose home Jesus was anointed with oil

When Martha heard that Jesus was coming, she went and met him. . . Jesus said to her, "I am the resurrection and the life. Those who believe in me, even though they die, will live, and everyone who lives and believes in me will never die. . . ."

John 11:20-26

(Matt. 26:6-13; John 12:1-8). He apparently visited here and stayed often. It was here that Jesus showed Mary and Martha the ways of the Kingdom of God (Luke 10:38-42).

Since Bethany played an important role in the ministry of Jesus, Christians throughout the ages have stressed its significance particularly in the Byzantine and Crusader eras. They erected grand churches above the tomb of Lazarus and over the location of Mary's and Martha's home. Today, modern churches stand near the remains of their ancient counterparts displaying their beautiful mosaics. On the facade of the Franciscan church known as the **Church of St. Lazarus** three ornate mosaics portray Mary, Martha and Lazarus.

Jerusalem

"The Holy City," "City of the Prophets," "City of Peace."
Jerusalem, the blessed city with a hundred names, is the only city in the world considered sacred by Jews, Christians and Muslims.

In his final days Jesus stayed in Jerusalem and the villages surrounding it. He prayed on the Mount of Olives. He taught in the Temple. He thrilled the masses who gathered to acclaim him the long-awaited Messiah. On the cobbled stones of Jerusalem Jesus walked his last steps. Here he was crucified. From the Mount of Olives Jesus ascended into heaven with the promise that he would come again.

Jesus experienced Jerusalem in all its glory. It was a beautiful, fortified city surrounded by walls. The Second Temple still stood. Built originally by Zerubbabel in the sixth century B.C. and renovated under Herod the Great, the glory of the Second Temple was never to be surpassed.

To the Jews, Jerusalem, "Yerushalayim" in Hebrew, symbolized their past and represented their hopes for the future. Known as the City of David and Mt. Moriah, the stories of David's exploits and Abraham's near sacrifice of Isaac filled the hopeful imagination of the faithful. Solomon's temple had stood on the mount. It had been destroyed by the Babylonians in the sixth century B.C.; yet the Second Temple had replaced it in the hearts of the people.

For Muslims, Jerusalem is one of their sacred cities. Several Muslim traditions are linked to it. The Muslims identify Jerusalem as the place where the Prophet Muhammad is believed to have ascended to heaven.

Jerusalem enjoys a splendid past and a present rich in the hope of a future peace which will spread throughout the earth. Many songs and poems have been written in its honor. Many people have praised it. Today many faithful believers around the world pray for the peace of this city. In Jerusalem the stones cry out with a story of splendor and destruction, of pain and ultimate victory.

Young woman's sandals from the Judean Desert caves, Bar Kokhba Revolt (A.D. 132-135). Display in Reuben and Edith Hecht Museum, University of Haifa.

"Hosanna!
Blessed is the one who comes in
the name of the Lord --
the King of Israel!"
John 12:13

The Triumphal Entry of Jesus into Jerusalem - Palm Sunday

When they were approaching Jerusalem, at Bethphage and Bethany, near the Mount of Olives, he sent two of his disciples and said to them, "Go into the village ahead of you, and immediately as you enter it, you will find tied there a colt that has never been ridden; untie it and bring it. If anyone says to you, 'Why are you doing this?' just say this, The Lord needs it and will send it back here immediately.'" They went away and found a colt tied near a door, outside in the street. As they were untying it, some of the bystanders said to them, "What are you doing, untying the colt?" They told them what Jesus had said; and they allowed them to take it. Then they brought the colt to Jesus and threw their cloaks on it; and he sat on it. Many people spread their cloaks on the road, and others spread leafy branches that they had cut in the fields. Then those who went ahead and those who followed were shouting,

"Hosanna!
Blessed is the one who comes in the name of the Lord!
Blessed is the coming kingdom of our ancestor David!
Hosanna in the highest heaven!"
Then he entered Jerusalem and went into the temple.

Mark 11:1-11

The Mount of Olives

The Mount of Olives is one of the most important sites around Jerusalem. It played a central role in the life of Jesus. He came here often. From this hill he prophesied to his disciples that the Temple would one day fall (Luke 19:41-44). After he celebrated his last supper with his followers, he went out to Gethsemane at the foot of the Mount of Olives to pray (Mark 14:26-42). Judas arrived with a company of officials and soldiers to arrest Jesus near the garden (John 18:1-12). From the summit of the mount Jesus ascended into heaven (Acts 1:6-12).

The name, Mount of Olives, derives from the olive groves that cover the hill east of the Old City of Jerusalem across the Kidron Valley; some of these groves can still be seen today. The mountain provides a buffer zone between the Judean Desert and the city of Jerusalem. The view from the top of the mountain is spectacular. East of the summit lies the Judean Desert. Looking west one can see an incredible view of the Old City and the rest of Jerusalem in all its glory.

The Mount of Olives is mentioned many times in the Old Testament. When Absalom revolted against his father David, the king fled to the Mount of Olives where he prayed to God (2 Sam. 15:30-31). There also King Josiah defiled the high places which King Solomon had built for the gods of the Moabites and Ammonites (2 Kings 23:13)

In Babylon Ezekiel had a vision of God's glory departing the Temple and stopping over *"the mountain east of the city"* (Ezek. 11:23).

Likewise Zechariah envisioned a day of great suffering for Jerusalem in which the Mount of Olives figures prominently (Zech. 14:1-5). Indeed the Mount of Olives and the Kidron Valley with the Valley of Jehoshaphat figure significantly in Jewish hopes for redemption and resurrection (e.g., Joel 2:30-3:3). The slope of the mount contains the world's oldest and largest Jewish cemetery.

The Churches on the Mount of Olives

Over the years many churches have been built commemorating the important events in Jesus' life that occurred on the Mount of Olives. The churches that tourists visit today were all built over structures initially erected during the Byzantine and Crusader periods. In recent times these have been renovated. The newer buildings have been constructed to complement the previous structures and to integrate the old with the new.

The Ascension into Heaven

[Jesus said] "But you will receive power when the Holy Spirit has come upon you; and you will be my witnesses in Jerusalem, in all Judea and Samaria, and to the ends of the earth." When he had said this, as they were watching, he was lifted up, and a cloud took him out of their sight. While he was going and they were gazing up toward heaven, suddenly two men in white robes stood by them. They said, "Men of Galilee, why do you stand looking up toward heaven? This Jesus, who has been taken up from you into heaven, will come in the same way as you saw him go into heaven." Then they returned to Jerusalem from the mount called Olivet, which is near Jerusalem, a sabbath day's journey away.

Acts 1:8-12

The Chapel of the Ascension

The peak of the Mount of Olives is considered the site of the ascension. Since the fourth century A.D. several churches have been erected on the summit in celebration of Jesus' ascension into heaven. In 378, the matron Poemenia founded the Church of the Ascension on this site. It was destroyed by the Persians in 614.

The chapel which guests enter today preserves the main features of the Crusader building. It was built originally with a reinforced outer wall and was protected by a fortress. In the center of the court the Crusaders built a small holy building surrounded by arched columns. These supported an open dome that sheltered a rock with a celebrated footprint of Christ. After the Crusaders were defeated in the twelfth century, the Muslims took over the building and turned it into a mosque. They closed the dome and built walls between the columns; yet the original Crusader building still stands today.

The rock inside the chapel with a celebrated footprint of Christ

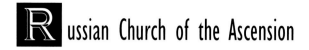 Russian Church of the Ascension

The Russian Orthodox church dedicated to the ascension of Jesus stands out because it has the tallest spire in the area and as such is one of the landmarks of the Mount of Olives. The church is built on the remains of a Byzantine church honoring John the Baptist. Some impressive mosaics remain from that period.

Lutheran Church of the Ascension "Auguste-Victoria"

The structure was commissioned by the German Emperor, Wilhelm II and his wife Empress Auguste-Victoria and built in 1907. It was originally erected as a complex including a hospice for pilgrims and the Church of the Ascension. Over the years the guest house was transformed into a hospital and afterwards into a clinic. Today the complex is managed by the Lutheran World Federation.

The site is called the Center for Pilgrims and Tourists and is operated by the "Foundation of the Empress Auguste-Victoria."

The Lutheran Church of the Ascension is situated on one of the highest points in Jerusalem, more then 800 m (2624 ft) above sea level. It contains beautiful mosaics and paintings depicting aspects of the life of Jesus. The mosaic in the apsis represents Christ ascending to heaven on a cloud. Its unique organ was built in 1910, designed by a German company, and is maintained today in its original condition.

Viri Galilea

Viri Galilea is Latin for "Men of Galilee" and refers to the messengers' address to Jesus' disciples on the occasion of the ascension (Acts 1:9-12). The Greek Orthodox built a church on the site. In one of the most significant ecclesiastical events of this century, Pope Paul VI met here with Athenagoras, the Greek Orthodox patriarch, in 1964.

Church of the Pater Noster

One of the panels, in Hebrew, displays the text of the Lord's Prayer.

> He said to them,"When you pray, say:
> Father, hallowed be your name.
> Your kingdom come.
> Give us each day our daily bread.
> And forgive us our sins,
> for we ourselves forgive
> everyone indebted to us.
> And do not bring us to the time
> of trial."
>
> Luke 11:2-4

In the Grotto of the Teaching, Jesus taught his disciples the Lord's Prayer, the "Pater Noster" (Latin for "Our Father"). Among the churches built here over the centuries, the first was erected during the fourth century A.D. Built by the Emperor Constantine and his mother, Helena, this large and imposing structure commemorated the ascension of Jesus and his teachings to his disciples regarding the last days. The name of the church was the same as the Greek name for olives, i.e., Eleona.

The modern church is run by the Carmelite nuns.

In the courtyard beautiful ceramic panels display the text of the Lord's Prayer in many languages.

The Cloister of the Church of the Pater Noster

Dominus Flevit

On the descent from the Mount of Olives towards Jerusalem stands a Franciscan church of unique architectural form; its dome is shaped like a tear. The altar faces Jerusalem as Jesus would have seen it when he first drew near to the city and wept over it. Thus it is called "Dominus Flevit" – "The Lord Wept."

When the church was being built, workers unearthed the remains of a church, built in Byzantine style, from the seventh century A.D.

Next to the church a large ancient cemetery was uncovered. It included several tombs from the Second Temple period. Impressive carved sarcophagi (stone coffins), ossuaries (stone boxes used to store human bones) and pottery were found. Altogether there were forty-three inscriptions bearing names such as Simeon, Maria and Jeshua. Some were engraved with a small cross next to its name. The excavators believed the site to have been a burial ground for Jewish Christians.

Russian Church of St. Mary Magdalene

Gold-plated, onion-shaped domes and spires characterize the Russian Church of Mary Magdalene and make the building visible from many miles away. Constructed in 1885-1888 by the Russian Czar Alexander III to honor his mother Maria, and named after St. Mary Magdalene, it is maintained today by Russian Orthodox nuns. The church's garden contains a set of stairs, one part of the ancient path leading to the summit of the Mount of Olives.

Gethsemane

When they had sung the hymn, they went out to the Mount of Olives. Then Jesus said to them, "You will all become deserters because of me this night. . . . " Then Jesus went with them to a place called Gethsemane; and he said to his disciples, "Sit here while I go over there and pray." He took with him Peter and the two sons of Zebedee, and began to be grieved and agitated. Then he said to them, "I am deeply grieved, even to death; remain here, and stay awake with me." And going a little farther, he threw himself on the ground and prayed, "My Father, if it is possible, let this cup pass from me; yet not what I want but what you want." …Then he came to the disciples and said to them, "Are you still sleeping and taking your rest? See, the hour is at hand, and the Son of Man is betrayed into the hands of sinners. Get up, let us be going. See, my betrayer is at hand."

Matthew 26:30-46

At the foot of the Mount of Olives, just above the Kidron Valley, stood the garden of Gethsemane, filled with olive trees. According to the Gospels, Jesus knew Gethsemane well because he *"often met there with his disciples"* (John 18:2; see also Luke 22:39). Jesus spent his last hours in solitude here; shortly afterward, he was captured by the Romans nearby.

The olive trees in the Garden of Gethsemane

The Mount of Olives with the Church of Gesthemane in the foreground

While he was still speaking, suddenly a crowd came, and the one called Judas, one of the twelve, was leading them. He approached Jesus to kiss him; but Jesus said to him, "Judas, is it with a kiss that you are betraying the Son of Man?" . . . Then Jesus said to the chief priests, the officers of the temple police, and the elders who had come for him, "Have you come out with swords and clubs as if I were a bandit? When I was with you day after day in the temple, you did not lay hands on me. But this is your hour, and the power of darkness!"

Luke 22:47-53

Today in Gethsemane visitors to the garden see the **Gethsemane Basilica**, a Franciscan church which is one of the most beautiful in Jerusalem. Next to it is the **Garden of Gethsemane** where the old olive trees grow and the **Grotto of Gethsemane.**

The Franciscan Grotto of Gethsemane
The Grotto of the Betrayal

The traditional Rock of the Agony lies in front of the main altar

The church of Gethsemane is also called the **Church of All Nations.** The dome bears symbols of the many nations which took part in its construction in 1924. Some know it as "The Basilica of the Agony." Inside the dome starlike lights are scattered to recreate the somber atmosphere, reminding all of the deep sorrow Jesus felt when he prayed here. The traditional Rock of the Agony lies in front of the main altar. The present floor of the church is designed in geometric shapes in a floral motif. It is similar to a Byzantine mosaic floor found on the site, which has also been incorporated into the design. Stones from the church of St. Saviour, which stood here during the Crusader period, have also been integrated into the new church.

The facade of the church consists of an enormous mosaic, one of the church's most memorable features. At its center Jesus prays all alone. Above this are the Greek letters Alpha and Omega, which recall Rev. 1:8: "'*I am the Alpha and the Omega,' says the Lord God, who is and who was and who is to come, the Almighty.*" On top of the facade are the sculptures of two deer, as Ps. 42:1 declares: "*As a deer longs for flowing streams, so my soul longs for you, O God.*"

The facade of Gethsemane Church

Church of the Tomb of the Virgin Mary

Situated at the foot of the Mount of Olives in the Kidron Valley, the church contains the traditional tomb of the Virgin Mary and commemorates her assumption. Built and maintained by Orthodox Christians, this church integrates the remains of earlier churches. The first church was built here at the end of the fourth century A.D., when the Tomb of the Virgin Mary was cut from the surrounding rock. During the Crusader period a monastery and a hostel for pilgrims were added. The complex was surrounded by a wall which made it look like a castle.

The church has a special atmosphere. The entrance through the Crusaders' well-preserved facade leads down many stairs to the lower level. In the center of the lower level is the Holy Tomb of the Virgin Mary.

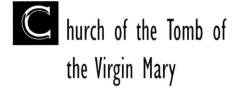

ther Sites on the Mount of Olives and its Environs

Absalom Tomb, Kidron Valley

The Jewish Cemetery

The largest and most ancient Jewish cemetery in the world begins near "the Valley of Jehoshaphat," a part of the Kidron Valley. It continues up to the summit of the Mount of Olives.

Many Jews came to Jerusalem in order to die and be buried in this cemetery.

The Tombs of the Prophets

Ancient tombs near the road from the Mount of Olives to Gethsemane mark the traditional burial places of the prophets Haggai and Malachi. As was customary, the tombs are hewn in the rock with niches and grottos connecting them.

Kidron Valley

The Kidron Valley separates the Mount of Olives from the Temple Mount and the Old City of Jerusalem. It leads to Mount Zion, the traditional site of the Last Supper and the house of Caiaphas, the high priest who examined Jesus before his crucifixion. In his comings and goings to the temple, to Gethsemane and to Bethany, Jesus crossed over the Kidron Valley many times.

Ancient tombs dot the landscape along the sides of the valley. The traditional sites of the tombs of Absalom, Zechariah, Jehoshaphat, and Bene Hezir (generally identified as St. James' tomb) are found here. Visitors are impressed by monuments that have been carved from indigenous rock and include pillars with capitals and stone carvings. Some Jews, Christians and Muslims believe that this will be the site of the final judgment ("the Valley of Jehoshaphat" – Joel 3:2). Because of this, the Kidron Valley has been a favorite burial place since the early days of Jerusalem.

The Jewish Cemetery, Mount of Olives with view of the Old City

Mount Scopus

Mount Scopus is the northern most peak of the Mount of Olives range. As the name suggests ("Ha-Tzofim" in Hebrew means "to look over") it offers a beautiful view of the Temple Mount in the Old City of Jerusalem. On another portion of the hill stand some of the

buildings that belong to the **Haddassah Hospital Medical Center** and part of the campus of the **Hebrew University**. Next to the Haddassah Hospital is a World War I cemetery where many British Soldiers are buried.

Because of its strategic location, Mount Scopus has played a decisive role in many battles for Jerusalem over the centuries. During the 1949 cease-fire Mount Scopus became an Israeli-held enclave in Jordanian territory. It reunited with the rest of the city in 1967.

The Jerusalem Center For Near Eastern Studies
Brigham Young University

The Mormon Center for Near Eastern Studies sits on one of the slopes leading up to the Mount of Olives and Mount Scopus. Beautifully kept gardens, court-yards, domes and arches - all faced with Jerusalem limestone - blend with the tra-ditional architectural style of the area. Sponsored by Brigham Young University

in Provo, Utah, the facility was established to provide students and scholars an opportunity to study the Bible in the land of its origin. Organized

tours are available for visitors and include a spectacular organ recital in the auditorium that overlooks the Old City of Jerusalem.

The Place of St. Stephen's Martyrdom

According to the New Testament, Stephen was the first Christian martyr, stoned to death because of his religious convictions (Acts 6-7). Two churches in Jerusalem are dedicated to him. One is the Greek Orthodox church located in the Kidron Valley, south-east of the Lion's Gate, known also as St. Stephen's Gate. The other is next to the Dominican Ecole Biblique (Catholic) north of the Old City of Jerusalem, near the present day Damascus Gate.

St. Stephen's Greek Orthodox Church

ount Zion

Mount Zion today refers to the hill southwest of the old City outside the Zion gate. Although it now lies outside the city walls, the area was previously enclosed. This area contains some of the most important sites in Jerusalem and has always been an important point of interest for visitors.

The spire of the Dormition Abbey on Mt. Zion adorns the sky of Jerusalem.

The Upper Room - The Room of the Last Supper

Jesus sent Peter and John into Jerusalem to make preparations for his last meal with his disciples. They were to find a man carrying a water jar and inquire where they could meet. Jesus told them: *"'He will show you a large room upstairs, already furnished. Make preparations for us there.'"* (Luke 22:12).

Mosaic depicting the "Last Supper," located in the Church of St. Peter in Gallicantu, Mt. Zion.

When the hour came, he took his place at the table, and the apostles with him. He said to them, "I have eagerly desired to eat this Passover with you before I suffer; for I tell you, I will not eat it until it is fulfilled in the kingdom of God." Then he took a cup, and after giving thanks he said, "Take this and divide it among yourselves; for I tell you that from now on I will not drink of the fruit of the vine until the kingdom of God comes." Then he took a loaf of bread, and when he had given thanks, he broke it and gave it to them, saying, "This is my body, which is given for you. Do this in remembrance of me." And he did the same with the cup after supper, saying, "This cup that is poured out for you is the new covenant in my blood. But see, the one who betrays me is with me, and his hand is on the table. For the Son of Man is going as it has been determined, but woe to that one by whom he is betrayed!"
Luke 22:14-22

The Upper Room, also known as coenaculum or cenacle, is the place where Jesus celebrated his final Passover with his disciples. His followers apparently assembled there at other times as well following Jesus' resurrection. According to the Gospel of John, Jesus appeared to his disciples on two occasions when his followers were assembled there, once without Thomas present and the other specifically to address Thomas' doubts that Jesus had indeed risen from the dead (John 20:19-29). This was also the room where the disciples gathered to replace Judas (Acts 1:15-26). Not long after, the gift of the Holy Spirit came upon believers who were gathered here on the day of Pentecost (Acts 2).

> *When the day of Pentecost had come, they were all together in one place. And suddenly from heaven there came a sound like the rush of a violent wind, and it filled the entire house where they were sitting. Divided tongues, as of fire, appeared among them, and a tongue rested on each of them. All of them were filled with the Holy Spirit and began to speak in other languages, as the Spirit gave them ability.*
>
> Acts 2:1-4

In the Byzantine period an enormous church stood on the traditional site of the Last Supper, known as "Holy Zion." It was one of the most important churches in Byzantine Jerusalem. The Medeba (Madaba) map, a mosaic floor map from the sixth century A.D., shows this church in the southern part of Jerusalem. Known as the "Mother of all Churches," it also marks the spot where the Apostles gathered.

In the Crusader period the large Church of St. Mary of Mt. Zion (Our Mother of Mount Zion) was built on the Byzantine church. The archaeological remains indicate that the church was quite large, approximately 72m (236 ft) by 36 m (118 ft).

The Upper Room today is a part of the Crusader church with later constructions. During the Ottoman period Muslims took over the structure and converted the room into a mosque. In the process they changed the original shape. Below this room is the traditional burial tomb of King David.

The traditional room of the Last Supper

(**The Syrian Church of St. Mark** in the Old City of Jerusalem is dedicated to St. Mark and to the site of the Upper Room. In addition it commemorates the Holy Spirit's descent upon the disciples as well as the spot of Mary's baptism.)

Dormition Abbey

A Catholic church marks the spot where the Virgin Mary fell into her "eternal sleep" (dormitio). It is one of the largest and most magnificent modern churches in Jerusalem, built by the Benedictine Fathers in 1906. Its spire, conical roof and the tower can be seen from far away and act as a beacon to locate Mount Zion. The church's interior is very bright. On the upper part of the apse there is a golden mosaic of Mary with the baby Jesus. A circular mosaic surrounded by the signs of the Zodiac decorates the floor. A wooden and ivory effigy of the Virgin Mary asleep in death graces the crypt of the church.

Incorporated into the building are the remains of the previous churches that stood on the summit of the Mount: the Byzantine church of Holy Zion and the Crusader church of St. Mary of Mt. Zion (Our Lady of Mount Zion).

Exterior of Dormition Abbey

A golden mosaic of Mary with the baby Jesus in the apse of Dormition Abbey

The House of Caiaphas

They took Jesus to the high priest; and all the chief priests, the elders, and the scribes were assembled. . . . Then the high priest stood up before them and asked Jesus, "Have you no answer? What is it that they testify against you?" But he was silent and did not answer. Again the high priest asked him, "Are you the Messiah, the Son of the Blessed One?"
Jesus said, "I am; and
'you will see the Son of Man seated at the right hand of the Power',
and 'coming with the clouds of heaven.'"

Mark 14:53-62

During Jesus' examination, Peter was sitting outside in the courtyard. As Jesus had predicted, Peter denied three times that he knew his teacher; then the cock crowed (Matt. 26:69-75).

The Church of St. Peter in Gallicantu is a Catholic church dedicated to Peter's denials. The word "gallicantu" refers to the crowing of the cock. The modern church was built by the Augustinian Fathers of the Assumption. Several previous churches were built on this site. Remains of a Byzantine monastery and church were discovered on the grounds of the church. They were built on the ruins of a Second Temple period structure. It contains underground rooms which may have been used as guard houses and a prison.

Next to the church, archaeologists have uncovered steps cut into the hill which led to a path to the City of David, the Kidron Valley and Gethsemane. This is likely the path Jesus took on his way from the Upper Room to Gethsemane and then, on his way back, from Gethsemane to Caiaphas' house.

Located on the eastern slopes of Mount Zion, visitors to the Church of St. Peter in Gallicantu may enter the balconies and view the City of David, the Kidron Valley, the Temple Mount and the Mount of Olives.

The Armenian Church of Caiaphas is close to the Zion Gate. In the church's courtyard archaeologists found dwellings from the Second Temple period. Some of these have underground rooms and cellars. The remains of a Byzantine church and a Crusader chapel were also discovered. The Armenian patriarchs are buried in the cemetery next to the church.

Other Sites on Mount Zion and its Environs

Hinnom Valley

The Hinnom Valley lies south-west of Mt. Zion. The Bible says that idolatry and child sacrifice took place in this area (Jer. 7:31-32). *"Therefore the days are surely coming, says the LORD, when this place shall no more be called Topheth, or the valley of the son of Hinnom, but the valley of Slaughter"* (Jer. 19:6). The Hebrew name of the Valley, "Gei Ben Hinnom" ("Gehenna"), became synonymous with "Hell."

Down in the valley is the "Hakeldama" (Field of Blood) that was used as a cemetery for pilgrims to Jerusalem. According to the New Testament the chief priests purchased this property with the thirty pieces of silver returned by Judas and used it as a place to bury foreigners (Matt. 27:3-10).

The Hinnom Valley contains the **Monastery of St. Onuphrius,** named after the famous Egyptian hermit from the fourth century A.D.

Tomb of David

The Tomb of David is the traditional burial place of King David. It includes a large stone covered with an embroidered cloth and decorated with silver crowns and torah scrolls. During Muslim rule the tomb were taken over and turned into a mosque; the original shape has therefore been adapted for that purpose.

The traditional David's Tomb

ity of David

David's City, the matrix of the city of Jerusalem, has been inhabited continuously since the time of King David. Indeed the city of Jerusalem is mentioned in the Bible even earlier than David's era. It is recorded in connection with Melchizedek, King of Salem and *"priest of God Most High"* who blessed Abraham, assured him of victory over his adversaries, and received from him *"a tenth of everything"* (Gen. 14:18-20).

Over three thousand years ago David defeated the city's inhabitants, the Jebusites, and occupied ancient Jerusalem.

"Who sing idle songs to the sound of the harp, and like David improvise on instruments of music." Amos 6:5

> David had said on that day, *"Whoever would strike down the Jebusites, let him get up the water shaft to attack the lame and the blind, those whom David hates."* Therefore it is said, *"The blind and the lame shall not come into the house."* David occupied the stronghold, and named it the city of David. David built the city all around from the Millo inward. And David became greater and greater, for the LORD, the God of hosts, was with him.
>
> 2 Samuel 5:8-10

David brought to Jerusalem the Ark of the Covenant, symbol of the unity of the tribes and of the covenant between the people and God. He established Jerusalem as the capital and worship center of the God of Israel. Later he built an altar on what became the Temple Mount, where his son Solomon built the First Temple. The sanctity of Jerusalem, and in particular, the Temple Mount, is already inferred in the Book of Genesis with the story of the sacrifice of Isaac on one of the mountains of the land of Moriah, where Abraham built his altar (Gen. 22).

The remains of the City of David are south of the present wall of the Old City. The City of David was a hill at the junction of the Tyropoeon and Kidron Valleys. Later it extended over the Valley of Hinnom, to the west. Since it was quite hilly, the city's northern border was less well-defined.

In this area archaeologists have uncovered interesting artifacts from the time of the City of David and the Kings of Judah, as well as later periods. Thick walls and outer battlements encircled the city and the residential areas they contained. Some of the fortifications of the walled city were uncovered in the excavation. The Babylonian destruction of Jerusalem in 586 B.C. (2 Kings 25:8-12) is also evidenced in the excavation. A thick conflagration layer with ashes and destroyed buildings found in the area corroborates Nehemiah's description of the ruins in the City of David as he found them in his tour of the city some one hundred and forty years later (Neh. 2:11-17).

One of the most impressive discoveries was the water supply system built for the city. Over the centuries ancient engineers created systems whereby water from the **Gihon Spring** (later called the fountain of the Virgin Mary), which lay outside the city, could be carried inside. The prophet Nathan and the priest Zadok anointed Solomon and the people acclaimed him king at Gihon (1 Kings 1:38-45).

Warren's Shaft is one of the most ancient water supply systems in Jerusalem. It contains shafts and a subterranean tunnel which connected the city to the spring. It was named after the archaeologist who discovered it.

The water systems also included a series of canals for irrigating agricultural areas. Another system was the **Siloam Tunnel** which carried the Gihon water to a pool, where the water could be stored. Part of it was an open channel and the other part was cut in the rock as a tunnel.

A figurine of horse and rider from the First Temple period displayed in the Center for Study of Jerusalem in the First Temple Period.

Perhaps the most impressive is **Hezekiah's Tunnel.** It was dug during the reign of King Hezekiah (about 700 B.C.). It transported water from the Gihon Spring to a reservoir, the Pool of Siloam, which lay inside the city walls to protect the water supply from enemies (2 Chr. 32:30). The tunnel is 533 meters (1748 ft) in length. Workmen began tunneling from each end and met in the middle. A Hebrew inscription was marked on the site where the two tunnels met.

The Pool of Siloam is known from the New Testament story in which Jesus healed the blind man by spitting on the ground, making mud and placing it on his eyes. Jesus then sent the man to wash in the Pool of Siloam and the blind man was healed. Later Jesus' opponents questioned the man about how he was cured, and he pointed them to Jesus (John 9). In the fifth century A.D. Christians built a church over the pool. The Persians destroyed it in A.D. 614.

The City of David Archaeological Project; Directed by the late Prof. Yigal Shiloh.

#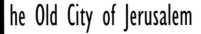

The Old City of Jerusalem may be likened to a thick book with each page another chapter in its history. In each period different people and rulers stamped their particular mark on the face of the city. With each change of government or culture it continued to evolve into the classic city it is today.

The walls that surround the Old City today were built during the Ottoman period by the Turkish sovereign, the Sultan Suleiman the Magnificent in the sixteenth century A.D. They are integrated with previous walls from different periods. Today, one enters the city through seven gates. An eighth gate - the Golden Gate - in the eastern wall of the Temple Mount was sealed by the Muslims many years ago.

The gates lead to the different quarters of the Old City: the Christian Quarter, the Armenian Quarter, the Jewish Quarter and the Muslim Quarter.

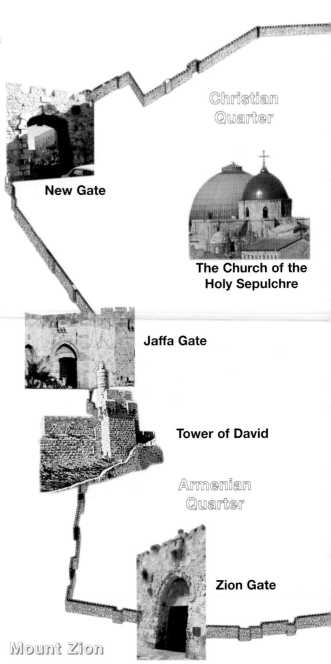

New Gate

Christian Quarter

The Church of the Holy Sepulchre

Jaffa Gate

Tower of David

Armenian Quarter

Zion Gate

Mount Zion

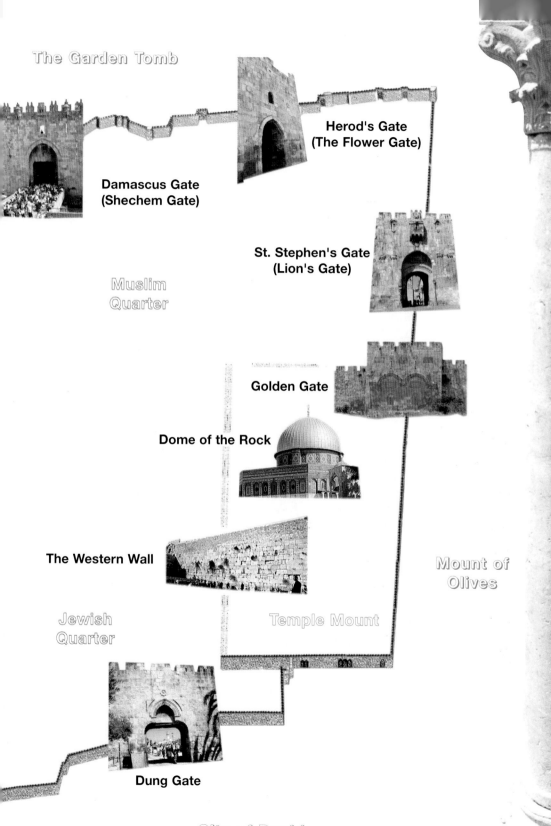

The Garden Tomb

Damascus Gate
(Shechem Gate)

Herod's Gate
(The Flower Gate)

Muslim
Quarter

St. Stephen's Gate
(Lion's Gate)

Golden Gate

Dome of the Rock

The Western Wall

Mount of
Olives

Jewish
Quarter

Temple Mount

Dung Gate

City of David

The Temple Mount

The story of Jesus begins at the Temple Mount. As Zecharias, the father of John the Baptist, served the Lord in the Temple, an angel appeared to him telling him of the imminent birth of his son (Luke 1:5-20). John would be the forerunner of the Messiah as the prophecies declared.

In Jesus' day, the Second Temple stood proudly on the crest of the mountain for all to see. Built originally in the sixth century B.C., the Temple Jesus entered had been renovated and enlarged by Herod the Great in the first century B.C.

Jesus visited the Temple Mount many times during his life. Forty days after his birth, Joseph and Mary brought him here *"to do for him what was customary under the Law"* (Luke 2:27). At the age of twelve he came with his parents to Jerusalem to celebrate the festival of the Jewish Passover. While there his parents lost track of him, but they found him days later in the Temple exchanging words of wisdom with Jewish teachers.

He asked them, *"'Why were you searching for me? Did you not know that I must be in my Father's house?'"* (Luke 2:49).

During Jesus' temptation experience the Devil brought Jesus to the Temple to test him and said,

> *"If you are the Son of God, throw yourself down from here, for it is written,*
> *'He will command his angels concerning you, to protect you,' and 'On their hands they will bear you up, so that you will not dash your foot against a stone.'"*
> *Jesus answered him, "It is said, 'Do not put the Lord your God to the test.'"*
>
> Luke 4:9-12

Immediately after the Triumphal Entry of Jesus into Jerusalem, he entered the Temple and drove out religious officials he accused of defiling the Temple.

Model of the Second Temple at the Model of Jerusalem next to Holyland Hotel, Jerusalem

Then they came to Jerusalem. And he entered the temple and began to drive out those who were selling and those who were buying in the temple, and he overturned the tables of the money changers and the seats of those who sold doves; and he would not allow anyone to carry anything through the temple. He was teaching and saying, "Is it not written, 'My house shall be called a house of prayer for all the nations'? But you have made it a den of robbers." And when the chief priests and the scribes heard it, they kept looking for a way to kill him.

Mark 11:15-18

But the final days of the Temple would be disastrous as Jesus warned in his prophecies:

When some were speaking about the temple, how it was adorned with beautiful stones and gifts dedicated to God, he said, "As for these things that you see, the days will come when not one stone will be left upon another; all will be thrown down."

Luke 21:5-6

The Gospels declare that when Jesus died, the veil of the Temple was torn from top to bottom (Matt. 27:51).

The History of the Temple Mount

In the biblical story the Temple Mount appears first as one of the mountains of the land of Moriah, the place where Abraham nearly sacrificed his son Isaac and built an altar (Gen. 22:2).

King David purchased the area from Araunah the Jebusite and erected there an altar to God (2 Sam. 24:16-25). Later both the First and Second Temples were built atop it (2 Chr. 3:1). According to Jewish tradition, this summit serves as the center of the world, the foundation of the entire universe.

David's son, King Solomon, erected the First Temple here and dedicated it in the tenth century B.C. Countless sheep and oxen were slaughtered there to mark the dedication (1 Kings 8:62). Construction of the temple lasted for seven years. The Palace Complex was built immediately to the south over a thirteen year period. During the invasion of Judah in 586 B.C., the Babylonians totally destroyed the splendid First Temple and took the chief citizens of Judah into exile (2 Kings 25).

Following the exile and after the Babylonians lost Judea to the Persians, the Persian King Cyrus gave permission for the exiles from the nations to return

Replica of the Ivory Pomegranate, First Temple Period.
Display in the Center for Study of Jerusalem in the First Temple Period.

Replica of a coin with the facade of the Temple, minted during Bar Kokhba Revolt against Rome (A.D.132-135).

home (538 B.C.). In addition, they allowed the Jews to start work on building the Second Temple. The Temple altar was repaired and the Temple implements restored. After some years, led by Zerubbabel and Jeshua (Ezra 3-4), the Jews built the Second Temple and dedicated it around 515 B.C.

During the Hasmonean period, the Seleucid ruler, Antiochus IV, declared Jerusalem a Greek "Polis," began to suppress the practices of Judaism, and eventually defiled the sacred site. The Jews, led by Judas Maccabaeus, rose in armed revolt. In 164 B.C. the Temple was purified and restored as the people's spiritual center (1 Macc. 4:36ff). This great victory of the Hasmoneans was and is still celebrated by the Jews in the feast of Hanukkah, known in John's Gospel as *"the Feast of Dedication"* (John 10:22).

In 37 B.C. Herod the Great, with Roman support, was declared King of Judea. Prior to Jesus' birth Herod began to renovate the Temple in grand style. He extended the foundation with a double esplanade, arched supports, and massive retaining walls. The Temple Mount and the Temple itself were impressive for the technology employed to build it, its splendor and its size. The beauty of the temple was repeatedly mentioned by Josephus and other historians; even the Rabbis said, "whosoever has not seen Herod's building [the Temple] has never seen a beautiful building" (Babylonian Talmud Bava Batra 4a). John's Gospel suggests the project took forty-six years to complete (John 2:20).

Replica of a silver coin minted at Jerusalem during the Jewish Revolt against Rome (A.D. 66-70).

However, the Second Temple lasted only to A.D. 70. Four years after the Jewish Revolt against Rome erupted, the Temple was destroyed by the Roman legions under the command of Titus. On the ninth of the Hebrew month of Av, much of the city went up in flames and the Temple burned in the fire. As Jesus had prophesied, not one stone was left upon the other in its destruction. The Menorah, the seven-branched candlestick, was taken by Titus to Rome.

During the second century A.D., around the time of the Bar Kokhba Revolt, the Romans rebuilt the city as a Roman colony, calling it "Aelia Capitolina." The Romans built their own pagan temple, dedicated to the god Jupiter, over the site of the Temple Mount. To add further insult they forbade the Jews from entering the holy city.

During the Byzantine era, after Christianity became the official religion of the empire, Jerusalem became a Christian city. The restoration of Jerusalem as a religious center led to an intensive construction of churches and other religious institutions, but the Temple Mount remained desolate as a reminder of Jesus' prophecy about it. (Mark 13:2).

Roman coin of the triumph over Judea, minted at Rome in A.D. 71. The Latin inscription reads: "JUDEA CAPTA." Display in the Bible Lands Museum, Jerusalem

The Temple Mount with the Dome of the Rock shining at night

In A.D. 614 the Persians conquered Jerusalem, burning many churches and monasteries. But shortly after in A.D. 628, Jerusalem was returned to Byzantine hands during the emperor Heraclius' reign, and some efforts were made to restore the city to its previous splendor.

Only ten years later, Jerusalem changed hands again, falling to the Muslim Arabs. The Caliph Omar identified the Temple Mount as the spot where the prophet Muhammad ascended into heaven, and thereafter the first mosque was built on the Mount.

Visitors to the Temple Mount today observe two impressive structures standing on the Temple Mount: the Dome of the Rock and the El Aqsa Mosque.

The Dome of the Rock is one of the most beautiful shrines in the Islamic world and one of the most exquisite landmarks in Jerusalem. It was built originally by the Umayyad Caliph 'Abd el Malik in A.D. 691-2. The golden dome was erected directly above the rock, where the Muslims believe the Prophet Muhammad ascended to heaven. It is surrounded by beautiful carpets, richly colored stained- glass windows and lovely mosaics. Much of the exterior decoration was redone over the centuries, but most of the interior decoration is original. This stone, octagonal building is the most ancient Muslim monument in the Holy Land.

Interior of the Dome of the Rock

El Aqsa Mosque, on the southern end of the Mount, was built after the Dome of the Rock. It was apparently begun by 'Abd el Malik and completed by his son, Walid I. The columns, ceiling, carpets and stained glass windows dominate the mosque's interior. While the Dome of the Rock has preserved its original plan and decoration, the El Aqsa Mosque is entirely different from what it was originally in the eighth century.

The Crusaders conquered Jerusalem in 1099. During the Crusader period and after the "King of Jerusalem" was crowned, the Temple Mount became a Christian site with a variety of religious traditions. The Christians converted the buildings on the Temple Mount into churches. But Christian dominance of the sites was short-lived. The buildings reverted to Arab use after the defeat of the Crusaders in 1187 and have remained Muslim holy places ever since. In Arabic they are called "El-Haram esh-Sharif" - "The Noble Sanctuary."

Replica of a Crusader coin minted at Jerusalem.

Underground stables used by the Crusaders, known traditionally as "Solomon's Stables."

The Dome of El Aqsa Mosque, and (below) an archaeological excavation from the Herodian Period

The **Archaeological excavations** at the base of the Temple Mount have produced some amazing finds from the First and Second Temple periods through the Ottoman period. From these discoveries it has been possible to reconstruct the Temple Mount during its various periods, including the location of its surrounding walls and entrances.

South of the Temple Mount the **Archaeological Garden Ophel** displayed most of the historical levels of Jerusalem. One can go on a splendid three-thousand-year tour into the past.

North of the Temple Mount in the **"West Wall Tunnels,"** archaeologists have uncovered the entire length of the western wall (approx. 500 m, 1650 ft) which enclosed the Herodian Temple Mount. The walls, whose lower parts functioned as retaining walls, were founded for their entire length on bedrock, following the local topography.

The Pools of Bethesda (Beth-Zatha)
The Church of St. Anne

Now in Jerusalem by the Sheep Gate there is a pool, called in Hebrew Beth-zatha, which has five porticoes. In these lay many invalids--blind, lame, and para-lyzed. One man was there who had been ill for thirty-eight years. When Jesus saw him lying there and knew that he had been there a long time, he said to him, "Do you want to be made well?" The sick man answered him," Sir, I have no one to put me into the pool when the water is stirred up; and while I am making my way, someone else steps down ahead of me." Jesus said to him, "Stand up, take your mat and walk." At once the man was made well, and he took up his mat and began to walk.

John 5:2-9

During the Byzantine and the Crusader eras Christians built large churches in honor of the healing of the paralytic. At the same time the churches commemorated Mary's birthplace, tradi-tionally located in this area.

The archaeological excavations of the Pools of Bethesda

The Pools of Bethesda near St. Stephen's (the Lion's) Gate were hewn in the bed of the Bezetha Valley. It is high-ly probable that they coincided with the Sheep's Pool of Second Temple times.

The two large pools were built origi-nally as part of a water supply system. Afterwards grottos were dug out to the east of the pools to provide a water cis-tern and baths for medical or religious purposes. The pools have been known as places of healing. Throughout history many have come to seek relief from their illnesses from these pools, which impress with their size. According to the Gospel of John it was here that Jesus met and healed the man who had been ill for thirty-eight years (John 5:2-9).

Today the **Church of St. Anne** stands next to the pools. It was built by the Crusaders around 1130 and dedicated to St. Anne, Mary's mother. The church, built in the Romanesque style, is one of the most beautiful Crusader churches in the Holy Land.

After the defeat of the Crusaders, Saladin turned the church into a school to foster the Islamic faith. In 1856, following the Crimean War, the Ottoman Turks presented the site to France in gratitude for their support during the war. The church was eventually restored to its former condition.

The Church of St. Anne

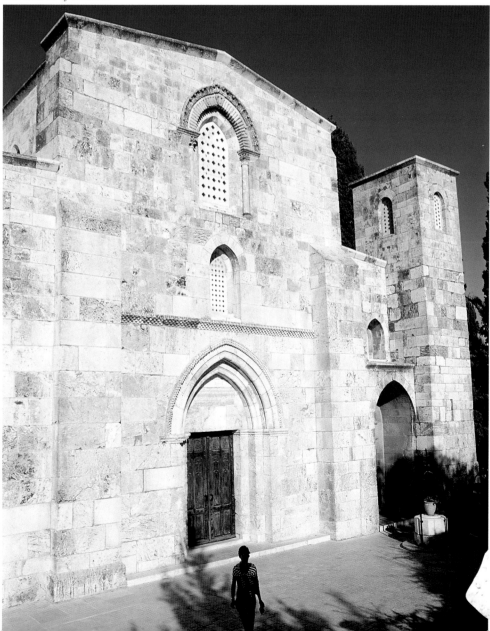

137

The Christian Quarter and the Via Dolorosa

The Christian Quarter lies in the north-west part of the Old City. In the center of the **Christian Quarter** stands the **Church of the Holy Sepulchre**. It lies along the path known as the **Via Dolorosa, "Way of Sorrow."** It is surrounded by churches, monasteries, administrative centers for various Christian denominations, charitable institutions and hostels for pilgrims who travel to the holy sites.

The Via Dolorosa marks the path Jesus traveled as he carried the cross from the place he was sentenced to the place of his crucifixion. The road of travail has fourteen traditional stations which mark events which transpired along Jesus' long, final walk to his execution.

When making the Stations of the Cross in Jerusalem today, one follows the route used since the Middle Ages. The first part passes through the Muslim

Quarter while the remainder goes through the Christian Quarter. Every Friday Christian pilgrims join the Franciscan procession to retrace Jesus' steps and recall his agony. For many the walk along the Via Dolorosa is one of the high points of a visit to the Holy Land, leaving them with an indescribable feeling of sorrow and joy.

The Stations of the Cross

First Station: the Place of the Condemnation

The traditional "praetorium," "the court of law," was located in the Fortress of Antonia which stood north of the Temple Mount. The fortress safeguarded the temple area and served as the headquarters for the Roman garrison securing the area. Adjacent to the Fortress are rooms that the Greek Orthodox identify as the prison where Jesus was held prior to the Crucifixion.

Today the Muslim school "Omariya" occupies the site. The building, established during the period of Turkish rule, had used the edifice for other purposes, especially military.

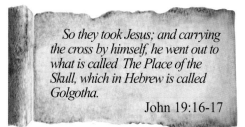

Franciscans in the courtyard of the "Omariya" school

Second Station: the Burden of the Cross

The second station of the cross is located in the Franciscan compound which contains the sanctuaries of the Condemnation and the Flagellation as well as a Franciscan center for research in religious studies and the Bible.

Chapel of the Flagellation

The Church of the Condemnation was built in the form of the Byzantine church which had stood there previously. Outside the church there is a stone which marks the beginning of the famous lithostrotos, the stone floor in the central courtyard of the Fortress of Antonia. This is the site where the Cross was placed on the shoulders of Jesus, who then carried it to the place of execution.

The Chapel of the Flagellation stands over the foundations of older churches. An interesting facet of the church are three stained-glass windows depicting different scenes: the washing of Pilate's hands from the guilt of Jesus' condemnation (Matt. 27:24); the scourging and crowning of Jesus with the crown of thorns (Matt. 27:27-31); the victory cry of Barabbas on his release (Matt. 27:26).

Church of the Condemnation

The "Ecce Homo" Arch and the Convent of the Sisters of Zion

> *So Jesus came out, wearing the crown of thorns and the purple robe. Pilate said to them, "Here is the man!"*
>
> John 19:5
>
> *When Pilate heard these words, he brought Jesus outside and sat on the judge's bench at a place called The Stone Pavement, or in Hebrew Gabbatha.*
>
> John 19:13

On this traditional spot Pontius Pilate presented Jesus to the crowds and said: "Behold the Man," in Latin, "Ecce Homo."

The present arch was actually part of a large triple-arched gateway to the Roman city Aelia Capitolina, built by the Emperor Hadrian in the second century A.D. Today the central arch spans the street, while the northern arch is incorporated into the church in the Convent of the Sisters of Zion (Sion).

The convent building was built by Alphonse Ratisbonne in 1857. In excavations done underneath the church, researchers have uncovered incredible evidence of what Jerusalem looked like in Roman times.

The central part of the Ecce-Homo Arch which spans the street.

Engraving of the "Basileus" game in a stone floor found in the archaeological excavation inside the Convent of the Sisters of Zion.

One of the most interesting finds was an engraving in the stone floor of the "king's game" played by the Roman garrison. The engraving is of the symbol "B" with a crown near it, denoting the word "Basileus" ("king" in Greek).

Inside the convent guests can view the impressive archaeological remains. The upper floor of the convent houses a hostel for pilgrims; from the roof of the convent visitors delight in a most incredible view of the Old City and its sights.

The northern part of the Ecce Homo Arch

Third Station: Jesus Falls for the First Time

The third station marks the spot where the tortured and exhausted Jesus fell under the weight of the cross for the first time. It is marked by a chapel built by Polish soldiers who arrived in Jerusalem during the Second World War. In the chapel's facade is a stone sculpture portraying the event of the Third Station. Today the Armenian Catholics manage the site.

Fourth Station: Jesus Meets His Mother

A relief carved in stone represents the place where Jesus met his mother during his final march toward death. Next door, in the Church of Our Lady of Spasm is a mosaic floor belonging to an earlier Byzantine church that stood on the premises. It has beautiful decorations, including one showing a pair of

sandals facing north. These sandals are also seen in a Christian lithograph from the fourteen century A.D. as the place where Mary stood suffering when she saw her son carrying the cross. The site is managed by the Armenian Catholics.

Fifth Station: Simon of Cyrene Helps Jesus

As they led him away, they seized a man, Simon of Cyrene, who was coming from the country, and they laid the cross on him, and made him carry it behind Jesus.

Luke 23:26

A Franciscan chapel built in the nineteenth century marks the site. The chapel is dedicated to Simon of Cyrene who helped Jesus carry the cross. From here the Via Dolorosa climbs toward Golgotha.

Opposite page: Christian pilgrims join the Franciscan weekly procession along the Via Dolorosa.

ixth Station: Veronica Wipes the Face of Jesus

According to tradition Jesus healed a woman named Veronica during his ministry. As a sign of her gratitude to Jesus, she accompanied him to the place of his execution. When she wiped his sweating face along the way, the imprint of his face remained on the cloth.

The church of St. Veronica cared for by "the Little Sisters of Jesus" lies on the site where Veronica is believed to have lived.

The site was acquired by the Greek Catholics in 1883. Underneath the site are remains of a church which may date back to the sixth century A.D.

eventh Station: Jesus Falls for the Second Time

This station indicates the traditional place where the Gate of Judgment stood. Here the authorities pronounced the judgments passed on those convicted of crimes. A Roman column, housed in a Catholic chapel, marks the place of Jesus' second fall while passing out of the city through this gate.

Eighth Station: Jesus Speaks to the Women of Jerusalem

A great number of the people followed him, and among them were women who were beating their breasts and wailing for him. But Jesus turned to them and said, "Daughters of Jerusalem, do not weep for me, but weep for yourselves and for your children. For the days are surely coming when they will say, 'Blessed are the barren, and the wombs that never bore, and the breasts that never nursed.' Then they will begin to say to the mountains, 'Fall on us'; and to the hills, 'Cover us.' For if they do this when the wood is green, what will happen when it is dry?"

Luke 23:27-31

This event is marked by a stone with a Latin cross on the wall of a Greek Orthodox church. Near the cross an inscription reads: "Jesus Christ the Victor."

Franciscan procession along the road

N inth Station: Jesus Falls for the Third Time

Tradition tells us that Jesus collapsed for a third time not far from where he would be crucified. A Roman column indicates the location of his third and final fall. It has been incorporated into the wall of a Coptic Church. During the Crusader period there was a large monastery here: the remains of it are still visible today. Close by on a large terrace one can see the roof of St. Helena's Chapel (a part of the Church of the Holy Sepulchre) where a community of Abyssinian monks lives today.

Above: Franciscan nun at Friday Procession
Below: View of the Christian Quarter

Church of the Holy Sepulchre

After the Emperor Constantine converted to Christianity and published his edict tolerating the practice of the Christian faith, he and his mother, Helena, erected the first church on this site (fourth century A.D.). According to imperial order the church would be large and beautiful. The original structure was destroyed during the Persian invasion in A.D. 614, but was renovated after the victory of Emperor Heraclius over the Persians in A.D. 628. Yet it survived only to be demolished by the Muslims in the eleventh century. The only portions of the first building to endure were those excavated from the rock, namely, the Golgotha mound and the sepulchre itself.

In the same century the Emperor Constantine Monomachus directed the repair work of the ruined edifice. When the Crusaders arrived in the city in 1099, they altered the shape of the building and enlarged it. They decorated it with many elaborate mosaics and stone carvings.

This complex of buildings forms the basis of what we still see today. In the center of the complex rests the Holy Sepulchre; above it a magnificent rotunda with its marvelous dome highlights the spot. Next to it is the mound of Golgotha (Calvary). Below Golgotha is the Chapel of Adam, built in honor of the first man. At the entry to the church lies the anointment stone where, as tradition has it, Jesus' body was laid prior to its burial. Within the church complex many important chapels provide places of worship.

The building is shared by many Christian denominations, including Catholics, Greek Orthodox, Armenians, Syrians and Copts, while the Abyssinians occupy a portion of the roof.

Exterior of the Church of the Holy Sepulchre

The Stations of the Cross within the Holy Sepulchre

Tenth Station: Jesus Stripped of His Garments

The tenth station recalls that the Roman soldiers stripped Jesus of his clothing and gambled for his robe near where Jesus was crucified (John 19:23-25). Visitors can peer into the Latin chapel through a special window.

Eleventh Station: Jesus Nailed to the Cross

On the crest of Golgotha (Calvary) a beautiful Latin shrine marks the spot where soldiers nailed Jesus' hands and feet to the cross. A beautiful silver altar, a present from the Duke of Tuscany, describes the suffering of Christ in classic Renaissance style. A magnificent mosaic decorates the place above it. The ceiling contains a portion of a Crusader mosaic of the figure of Jesus; it once decorated the entire chapel.

149

Twelfth Station: Jesus Dies on the Cross

On Golgotha (Calvary) a Greek Orthodox altar, with a silver disc under it, marks the place of the crucifixion. On both sides of the altar are impressions which mark the locations where the Romans crucified the thieves together with Jesus (Mark 15:27). The bedrock beneath is the original rock of Golgotha which goes down to the foundation of the Chapel of Adam. The rock beneath contains a large crack caused by the cosmic events which accompanied Jesus' death: *"The earth shook, and the rocks were split"* (Matt. 27:51).

Thirteenth Station: Jesus is taken down from the Cross

The thirteenth Station marks the event when Jesus was taken down from the cross, while the Virgin Mother stood nearby. Upon a Franciscan altar dedicated to the Virgin Mary sits a statue of the Madonna brought from Lisbon in 1778 - the "Mater Dolorosa" – "Our Lady of Suffering." It is decorated with a golden crown and precious gifts from pilgrims.

After Joseph of Arimathea took Jesus down off the cross, Jesus was laid on the Stone of the Anointment, which lies at the entry to the church.

The Stone of the Anointment

Below: The Stations of the Cross on Golgotha (Calvary) inside the Holy Sepulchre

Fourteenth Station: The Burial and Resurrection of Jesus

The burial and resurrection site serves as the focal point of the church. The Tomb of Christ is inside a small enclosure in the center of the rotunda. Above the entrance of the Sepulchre is a relief depicting Jesus conquering death and rising from the Tomb. It has two chambers: The Chapel of the Angel and the Holy Sepulchre. The sacred rock of the Tomb is covered with marble and above it are paintings depicting the Resurrection.

Interior of the Holy Sepulchre

Entrance to the Holy Sepulchre
Inset left: The remodeling of the Rotunda above the Holy Sepulchre,
which was introduced to the public on Christmas Day, 1996.

And when they came to a place called Golgotha (which means Place of a Skull), they offered him wine to drink, mixed with gall; but when he tasted it, he would not drink it. And when they had crucified him, they divided his clothes among themselves by casting lots; then they sat down there and kept watch over him. Over his head they put the charge against him, which read, "This is Jesus, the King of the Jews."
Matthew 27:33-37

Then Jesus said, "Father, forgive them; for they do not know what they are doing." Luke 23:34

When it was noon, darkness came over the whole land until three in the afternoon. At three o'clock Jesus cried out with a loud voice, "Eloi, Eloi, lema sabachthani?" which means, "My God, my God, why have you forsaken me?" Mark 15:33-34

Then Jesus cried again with a loud voice and breathed his last. At that moment the curtain of the temple was torn in two, from top to bottom. The earth shook, and the rocks were split. Matthew 27:50-51

When it was evening, there came a rich man from Arimathea, named Joseph, who was also a disciple of Jesus. He went to Pilate and asked for the body of Jesus; then Pilate ordered it to be given to him. So Joseph took the body and wrapped it in a clean linen cloth and laid it in his own new tomb, which he had hewn in the rock. He then rolled a great stone to the door of the tomb and went away. Mary Magdalene and the other Mary were there, sitting opposite the tomb. Matthew 27:57-61

Roman soldiers crucified Jesus on a barren, rocky hilltop. In Aramaic it was called "Golgotha" ("Calvary" in Latin). It means the "place of a skull." Joseph of Arimathea provided a burial cave for Jesus adjacent to the place of his crucifixion; he sealed the entrance to the cave with a large stone. According to the New Testament, three days after he was crucified, God raised Jesus from the dead and the disciples found the tomb empty.

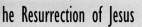

After the sabbath, as the first day of the week was dawning, Mary Magdalene and the other Mary went to see the tomb. And suddenly there was a great earthquake; for an angel of the Lord, descending from heaven, came and rolled back the stone and sat on it. His appearance was like lightning, and his clothing white as snow. For fear of him the guards shook and became like dead men. But the angel said to the women, "Do not be afraid; I know that you are looking for Jesus who was crucified. He is not here; for he has been raised, as he said. Come, see the place where he lay. Then go quickly and tell his disciples, 'He has been raised from the dead, and indeed he is going ahead of you to Galilee; there you will see him.' This is my message for you."

Matthew 28:1- 7

But Mary stood weeping outside the tomb. As she wept, she bent over to look into the tomb; and she saw two angels in white, sitting where the body of Jesus had been lying, one at the head and the other at the feet. They said to her, "Woman, why are you weeping?" She said to them, "They have taken away my Lord, and I do not know where they have laid him." When she had said this, she turned around and saw Jesus standing there, but she did not know that it was Jesus. Jesus said to her, "Woman, why are you weeping? Whom are you looking for?" Supposing him to be the gardener, she said to him, "Sir, if you have carried him away, tell me where you have laid him, and I will take him away." Jesus said to her, "Mary!" She turned and said to him in Hebrew, "Rabbouni!" (which means Teacher). Jesus said to her, "Do not hold on to me, because I have not yet ascended to the Father. But go to my brothers and say to them, 'I am ascending to my Father and your Father, to my God and your God.'"

John 20:11-17

The Garden Tomb and Resurrection Garden

The Garden Tomb is located outside the Old City walls, north of the Damascus gate. Despite the hustle and bustle of the city, it is beautifully manicured and possesses an air of tranquillity about it. From the Garden's viewing platform visitors can view the Old City and the walls around it.

Nearby is a barren knoll which, according to some, fits the description of Golgotha. It was out of the city gate but still near the city (John 19:20). The cliff of the barren knoll, near the Garden Tomb, is shaped like a skull, ("Golgotha" in Aramaic means "the place of the skull"). It also fits John's description: *"Now there was a garden in the place..."* (John 19:41). A large cistern and a wine press found in the garden indicates that the site has long been a garden.

Several caves found in the area contain skeletal remains, indicating that the area was once used for burial purposes. The Tomb in the Garden was hewn into the rock, a tombstone blocked the entrance. This evidence led some to believe that this may have been the site of Jesus' Tomb which Joseph of Arimathea gave for his burial after the crucifixion. On the door to the Tomb a sign reads: "HE IS NOT HERE—FOR HE IS RISEN."

The first person to identify the Garden Tomb (in 1883) was General Gordon, a British soldier and Bible student. In 1893 the Garden Tomb Association was founded and a year later the Tomb and Garden were purchased from their German owners. Since then the site has been cared for by the Association, which keeps it a quiet and sacred spot for praying and worshipping.

Right: The entrance of the Tomb
Below: The cliff of the barren knoll next to the Garden Tomb

The Armenian Quarter

The Armenian Quarter in the south-west corner of the Old City is the heart of the national, religious and cultural life of the Armenian Orthodox in Jerusalem.

In the middle of the walled Quarter is **St. James Cathedral,** the most important Armenian church in the Holy Land. The church is dedicated to St. James, the brother of St. John and one of the original "twelve." The New Testament tells us that he was executed by Herod Agrippa: *"About that time King Herod laid violent hands upon some who belonged to the church. He had James, the brother of John, killed with the sword"* (Acts 12:1-2).

Tradition holds that his head is buried here. The church also celebrates the life of St. James, Jesus' brother and the first bishop of Jerusalem, who is buried in the cathedral.

St. James Cathedral

Built on the foundation of a sixth century building and a Crusader church, this is one of the most impressive structures in Jerusalem. It is decorated with exquisite ornamentation, the handiwork of Armenian artists.

The Armenian Museum contains an outstanding collection of treasures belonging to the church as well as a library with a collection of old, hand-written manuscripts.

The Cloister of Deir El Zeitun (Olive Tree) and the Church of the Holy Archangels were built, according to one tradition, on the spot of the home of Annas, father-in-law of Caiaphas (John 18:13). A later tradition holds that Jesus was tied to an olive tree outside the chapel.

The courtyard of the Armenian Museum

The Jewish Quarter

The Jewish Quarter in the south-east part of the Old City, has been recognized as a center of Jewish spiritual life for hundreds of years. After the Six Day War in 1967, many archaeological excavations were made, which have increased greatly our understanding of the history of the city. The buildings in the Jewish Quarter were repaired, and the alleys and infrastructure were renewed. Guests of modern Jerusalem enjoy discovering how the old and the new blend together in so delightful a fashion.

The Ramban Synagogue is named after Rabbi Moshe Ben-Nahman, a thirteenth century Jewish Rabbi who revitalized the Jewish community in Jerusalem. He came to the Holy Land in 1267, and one of his first tasks was the construction of the synagogue in Jerusalem.

The Yochanan Ben Zakkai Four Sephardic Synagogues form a very old complex of synagogues that functioned as the spiritual center of the Sephardic Jewish community in Jerusalem. The Synagogues were built in the sixteenth century and restored, like all the Jewish Quarter, in 1967. The synagogues are still in use today.

The "Hurva" Synagogue of Rabbi Yehuda the Hassid has been used as a community center for the "Ashkenazi" Jews. It is named after Rabbi Yehuda the Hassid, who came to the Holy Land in A.D. 1700 and bought this land. In the nineteenth century it was the most elaborate synagogue in the Old City. So that visitors could understand its former glory, one enormous arch was reconstructed in 1967.

The reconstructed arch of the "Hurva" Synagogue in the Jewish Quarter

The Center for the Study of Jerusalem in the First Temple Period presents to guests a permanent exhibit showing life as it was in Jerusalem in the days of the Old Testament. Perhaps the most interesting part of the exhibit is the scale model of Jerusalem displaying the City of David and the later expansion of Jerusalem in the First Temple period, with its accompanying 3-D sound and light show.

The Herodian Quarter (The Wohl Archaeological Museum) contains the remains of homes built during the Second Temple era. The Upper City, as it was once called, included the houses of many wealthy people.

Here one can see the remains of painted walls (frescoes), mosaic floors, stone tables, stone vessels and Mikvehs (ritual baths). These indicate the high standard of living and religious observance that prevailed in this quarter during the Herodian period.

Another attraction from this period is **"The Burnt House."** It is part of a private home which had been burnt in the fire of Jerusalem after the destruction of the Second Temple in the year A.D. 70. Most tantalizing of the household artifacts found on this site are stone weights engraved with the name "Katros," a wealthy priestly family that served in the Temple and are mentioned in the Jewish Talmud. Further evidence of the consequences of the war on the household was provided by the bones of a young woman's hand and found against one of the walls.

Visitors can also see what is left of the **Cardo Maximus**, the main thoroughfare of the Roman-Byzantine city. This road is shown very clearly on a mosaic floor map from the sixth century A.D. found in the Jordanian town of Medeba (Madaba). At the center of the mosaic, Jerusalem is depicted as an oval, walled city with a colonnaded street running north-south, known as the Cardo Maximus. The archaeological ruins demonstrate how wide the Cardo was and that the roofed shops were erected originally on either side of the road. The street began at the Damascus gate of today. At the end of the Cardo one can visit a few ruins of the "Nea Church," which was built by the Byzantine Emperor Justinian during the sixth century A.D. On the upper level of the street the modern market of the "Cardo," with its fancy stores, comes alive today just as it did many years ago.

Ruins of the ancient "Cardo Maximus," the main road of Jerusalem in the Roman and Byzantine periods

The Holy City of Jerusalem, part of the Medeba (Madaba) Mosaic Map from the 6th Century A.D.

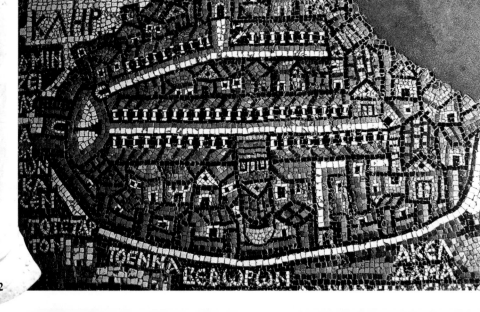

The Western Wall

The Western Wall may well be one of the most significant places in the Holy Land. It symbolizes the return of the people of Israel to the Land of Promise. Known also as "the Wailing Wall," it is truly one of the most sacred shrines for the Jews and a place for public worship and celebration.

The wall is a remnant of the Second Temple, built initially in the sixth century B.C. and enlarged by Herod the Great during the first century B.C. The Western Wall was a part of the retaining walls that once enclosed the Herodian Temple Mount. The original Herodian stones can still be identified.

Faithful pilgrims journey here from all over the world to pray and worship. According to Orthodox Jewish practice, men and women pray separately at the wall. Some write their prayers on small pieces of paper and slip them into the cracks between the large stones.

The Muslim Quarter

The Muslim Quarter lies in the northeast part of the Old City, adjacent to the Temple Mount and its Holy Muslim sites. It contains most of the markets and bazaars of the Old City, making a walk through the vibrant streets an interesting tourist experience. These covered markets are roofed by domes supported by pointed arches and are classified according to their wares. Each shop has its own special smell and unique atmosphere. The wares include: antiques, jewelry, perfume, embroideries, leather goods, meats, ethnic foods with special sweets and oriental spices, Arab cafes and a fruit juice bar. The list is endless.

The streets of the Muslim Quarter lead to the Temple Mount on which stands the Dome of the Rock and the El-Aqsa Mosque, the sacred shrines of the Muslims.

The Tower of David Museum - The Citadel

The Citadel, better known as the Tower of David, sits on the western hill of the city next to the Jaffa Gate. Because of its strategic position, the rulers of Jerusalem, beginning with the Hasmoneans in the second century B.C. and Herod the Great in the first century B.C., have fortified this place as a stronghold. The Muslim minaret, built by the Ottoman Turks, and the towers of the upper level are one of the well known landmarks in Jerusalem.

The resulting complex of buildings that constitute the fortress today unfolds for us the rich and varied history of the entire city. Today, a modern museum in the rooms of the tower uses holographic imaging and other current technology to take us on a fascinating journey through the ages. The courtyard contains a unique archaeological garden. During the summer months visitors can enjoy an audio-visual presentation that makes even the stones come alive with the story of Jerusalem. This collection spreads before us the full spectrum of the spellbinding history of Jerusalem.

The New City of Jerusalem

The newer parts of Jerusalem have developed outside the walls of the Old City and constitute a bustling metropolis. The first modern neighborhood built was west of Mount Zion and is known as **Mishkenot Sha'ananim.** It was founded in 1860 by Sir Moses Montefiore with the help of contributions from another benefactor, Yehuda Touro. A tour of its first homes and its artists' galleries is most interesting.

Since the establishment of Mishkenot Sha'ananim many more new neighborhoods have developed, making Jerusalem Israel's largest city. What makes these suburbs special is that they are spread out on the hills that surround the heart of the ancient city. Another factor adding to the unique beauty of the city is the Jerusalem stone used on the exterior of all the buildings. In this way modern Jerusalem safeguards the special character of its historic grandeur, making it one of the most beautiful cities in the world.

It is recommended that visitors take advantage of the panoramic views of the city from its eastern suburbs on Mount of Olives or Mount Scopus and from the southern suburb of Armon Hanatziv.

Flour mill used by the original residents of Mishkenot Sha'ananim neighborhood

The Knesset

The Knesset is Israel's parliament. It has one hundred and twenty members. The special building which houses the Knesset was established with funds from the family of James De Rothschild. The Knesset moved to its present location in 1966.

The Knesset

Nearby is the **Knesset Menorah** (the seven-branched candelabrum), the official symbol of the state of Israel. The Menorah, a gift from Britain to Israel, was created by the sculptor Benno Elkan. It is covered with images depicting special events in the annals of Israel's history.

 he High Court

The High Court occupies a most impressive building that combines modern architecture with symbols connected to justice and law. These symbols represent much of the history of the people of Israel.

G overnment Center

The Government Center houses most of the administrative offices of the government, including the offices of the Prime Minister.

The High Court Building

I srael Museum

The Israel Museum contains a wealth of archaeological treasures from Israel and the Middle East, ethnic collections and the world's largest collection of Judaica. It also contains exhibitions of Israeli and international art. In addition there is an activity center for youth, a rich library, an auditorium and an art garden.

The Youth Wing, Israel Museum

S hrine of the Book

Part of the Israel Museum is a separate building constructed especially to house the Dead Sea Scrolls. These scrolls were found in caves near the Dead Sea and Qumran. The facility also includes other ancient handwritten Hebrew scrolls found in the Judean Desert. They provide a firsthand account of life in Judea about two thousand years ago. The building's white dome resembles the lid of one of the earthenware jars in which the scrolls were hidden.

B ible Lands Museum

The Bible Lands Museum houses one of the world's most important collections tracing the cultures and civilizations which rose and fell in the ancient lands of the Bible. The exhibition contains priceless ancient artifacts dating from the Neolithic period (6000 B.C.) to the Byzantine period (A.D. 600). One can take a unique journey tracing the roots of religion at the same time experiencing life and society in the Bible Lands.

Church Chancel Screen, region of Gaza, 6th century A.D., in the Bible Lands Museum.

ockefeller Museum

The Rockefeller Museum was established during the time of the British Mandate in Israel (1922-1948). It was the first archaeological museum in the country. Many of the treasures on display were excavated in the Holy Land in the first half of this century. The exhibits demonstrate how the antiquities discovered connect to the various cultures in the Holy Land.

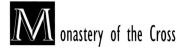onastery of the Cross

This well-preserved eleventh century monastery was named after the tradition that the tree from which Jesus' cross was made grew here. The massive structure, built like a fortress, stood in the Valley of the Cross above the ruins of a Byzantine monastery. The structure was built by Georgian monks. Today, the Greek Orthodox use the monastery.

odel of Jerusalem
Second Temple Period

Artisans have constructed a 1:50 scale model representing Jerusalem during the Second Temple period. It includes all the walls and fortifications, the public buildings, palaces, markets and homes. The "jewel in the crown" is the model of the Second Temple rebuilt by Herod the Great and destroyed by Titus in A.D. 70. The model was constructed as much as possible from the original materials used at the time: marble, stone, wood, copper and iron. The topography is an exact copy of Jerusalem during the time of Christ.

The Holyland Hotel maintains the Model.

The Jerusalem Windows - Chagall Windows

The synagogue of the new Hadassah-Hebrew University Medical Center in west Jerusalem, over looking Ein Kerem, houses twelve magnificent stained-glass windows. They were designed by the noted French Jewish artist Marc Chagall. The windows were commissioned by Hadassah, the Women's Zionist Organization of America. They symbolize the twelve sons of Jacob from whom came the twelve tribes of Israel. They recall the blessings bestowed on each son of Jacob and each tribe (Genesis 49, Deuteronomy 33).

Mea She'arim

Mea She'arim is one of the first neighborhoods built outside the walls of the Old City in 1874-5. The name Mea She'arim is Hebrew for "One Hundred Gates" and is taken from Genesis 26:12: *"Isaac sowed seed in that land, and in the same year reaped a hundredfold."*

The neighborhood was inhabited by eastern European Jews; today, Orthodox Jews make the area their home. The neighborhood is blessed with many synagogues, "yeshivas" and small prayer houses, all dedicated to prayer and the study of the Torah and its commentaries.

Pillar of Heroism, Yad Vashem

 **ad Vashem**

The Yad Vashem honors the victims of the Holocaust. It is also a research center and houses the central archives for research into the Holocaust. Its memorial section contains a special Hall of remembrance called in Hebrew "Ohel Yizkor," a memorial to the destroyed communities, the Children's Memorial, a permanent exhibit presenting the events of the Holocaust, and authentic objects from the ghettoes and concentration camps.

The Last March, Yad Vashem

 ount Herzl

Mount Herzl is a military cemetery and memorial to Benjamin Ze'ev Theodor Herzl who is buried here. Theodor Herzl was one of the founders of the Zionist movement to establish a Jewish homeland. In 1897 he convened the Zionist Congress at Basel, Switzerland. Mount Herzl is also the burial place of the founders of Israel and its leaders, including Levi Eshkol, Golda Meir, Ze'ev Jabotinski and Yitzhak Rabin, who was assassinated in 1995 while serving as Prime Minister of the State of Israel.

 live Columns Park

South of Jerusalem, near kibbutz Ramat Rahel, the "Olive Columns" Park is located. In the center of the site is a special sculpture, made by Ran Morin, that consists of three columns out of which grow three olive trees. The trees still bear fruit each year. The site also offers a spectacular view of Bethlehem and the Judean Desert.

Emmaus

Now on that same day two of them were going to a village called Emmaus, about seven miles from Jerusalem, and talking with each other about all these things that had happened. While they were talking and discussing, Jesus himself came near and went with them, but their eyes were kept from recognizing him. And he said to them, "What are you discussing with each other while you walk along?" They stood still, looking sad. Then one of them, whose name was Cleopas, answered him, "Are you the only stranger in Jerusalem who does not know the things that have taken place there in these days?" He asked them, "What things?" They replied, "The things about Jesus of Nazareth, who was a prophet mighty in deed and word before God and all the people . . . " So he went in to stay with them. When he was at the table with them, he took bread, blessed and broke it, and gave it to them. Then their eyes were opened, and they recognized him; and he vanished from their sight.

Luke 24:13-31

The Catholic Church dedicated to Cleopas' house in Qubeibeh

Several churches have been built to dedicate the occasion when Jesus appeared to Cleopas and his companion. It is clear that Emmaus was situated on a main route, leading from the west up to Jerusalem. Yet, different traditions led to several sites which people associated with the ancient Emmaus.

The archaeological site of ancient Emmaus is linked with the **Ayalon Valley (Aijalon Valley)**. The village's history goes back to the Hellenistic period when it was first known as "Emmaus." In the third century A.D., Emmaus was granted the status of a city and named Nicopolis. As its remains demonstrate, the town flourished during the Roman and Byzantine eras. Near the site one can see an interesting complex including the remains of a Roman villa, Byzantine churches with a baptistry and a twelfth-century Crusader church built in the prevailing Romanesque style.

The Ayalon valley is also famous as the battleground between the Amorites and Israelites on the day the sun stood still.

Joshua prayed:

"Sun, stand still at Gibeon, and Moon, in the valley of Aijalon."
And the sun stood still, and the moon stopped, until the nation took vengeance on their enemies.
Joshua 10:12-13

Another traditional site of Emmaus is the village of **Qubeibeh**, northwest of Jerusalem. This Arab village contains the remains of the ancient settlement from Old Testament and later periods. The most impressive are the finds from the Crusader village. These include a castle, a large church, public buildings and houses. In the center of the village stands an elaborate Catholic church dedicated to Cleopas' house; it integrates the ancient Crusaders' structures into the building you see today.

The archaeological site of ancient Emmaus in Ayalon Valley

The Crusader Church of Abu-Ghosh

One more possible site for Emmaus is the village of **Abu-Ghosh**, located west of Jerusalem. The location of the village is associated with Kiriath-jearim where the Ark of the Lord lodged prior to the establishment of the monarchy (1 Sam. 7:1). Today visitors can see its beautiful churches - old and modern - nestled between the hills of the village. On the summit of the village stands the beautiful church, Our Lady of the Ark of the Covenant. In the center of the village one can see the Crusader Church and Monastery, one of the country's best preserved and most attractive Crusader remains. The site is managed today by the Lazarist Fathers.

The Trappist Monastery of Latroun in Ayalon Valley belongs to the monastic order of St. Benedict. Situated on fertile land, the monastery is surrounded by olive groves, vineyards and fields of grain. The monastery is renowned for its excellent wine.

Other Sites in the Central Regions of the Holy Land

H ebron
Kiriath-arba; Mamre

Hebron is one of the oldest cities in the Holy Land. Its springs, its fertile lands, and its location on the main mountain route, brought many settlers to this region. The information about ancient Hebron comes from the Bible, where it is also called Kiriath-arba and Mamre. Located thirty-five km (22 miles) southwest of Jerusalem on some of the main thoroughfares in the territory, Hebron became famous for its association with Abraham: *"So Abram moved his tent, and came and settled by the oaks of Mamre, which are at Hebron; and there he built an altar to the LORD"* (Gen. 13:18).

God appeared in the form of three men to Abraham near the **Oaks of Mamre (Elonei Mamre)** in Hebron to announce that Sarah would have a son (Genesis 18:1-10).

Hebron remained an important city into the period of the monarchy. King David ruled Judah from Hebron for seven and one-half years before he made Jerusalem his capital (2 Sam. 2:11). Thereafter Hebron is frequently mentioned in later sources from the Hellenistic period through the Ottoman period. Hebron continues to be one of the most sacred cities in the Holy Land for the Jews alongside Jerusalem, Safed and Tiberias.

The Cave of Machpelah lies on a slope opposite the mound of Biblical Hebron. Abraham purchased the cave and its surrounding field from Ephron the Hittite as a burial place for Sarah (Gen. 23). It became the burial vault for the patriarchs and matriarchs of Israel. Abraham and his wife Sarah, Isaac and his wife Rebekah, and Jacob and his wife Leah are buried in Machpelah (Gen. 49:29-32).

The monument structure above the cave was built in the Second Temple period. It is commonly attributed to Herod the Great, although some scholars date it even earlier. Over the years the building has undergone various modifications and additions.

Exterior of the building above the cave of the Machpelah

H erodium (Herodion)

Herodium was a magnificent palace on the summit of a mount, south of Jerusalem. It was named for Herod the Great, its builder. It was built near the end of the first century B.C. as a fortified castle with a palace inside.

Herod had the original mound augmented, enlarging it and building a fortress atop it. It included two parallel circular walls with towers, residential rooms, a garden enclosed by columns and a well-built bath house. According to the historian Josephus, two hundred polished stone steps led to its summit. Some huge cisterns were found on the summit and on the interior of the hill.

On the north side of the hill there is a large excavation area known as Lower Herodium. This area includes remains of a garden surrounded by columns, a pool, monumental buildings, storage buildings and a bathhouse. Numerous remains from the Byzantine period including three small churches were also uncovered at Lower Herodium.

According to Josephus Herodium was built to serve as a fortress and center for the region, as well as a memorial to Herod. Josephus also gives us a full description of Herod's funeral procession to his burial place at Herodium (*Jewish Wars*). Yet his tomb has still not been found.

The palace played an important role during the Jewish Revolt against the Romans (A.D. 66-70) and during the Bar Kokhba Revolt (A.D. 132-135). The Zealots erected a synagogue, a ritual bath and some chambers to hide from the Romans.

The Monasteries of the Desert

Mar Saba Monastery

East of Jerusalem and Bethlehem the Judean Desert drifts down to the Jordan Valley. Although the desert may be small in size, its significance throughout recorded history has been enormous.

Despite the arid climate, the Judean wilderness has attracted many different peoples from ancient times. One of the most significant movements in the desert started in the fourth century A.D. The Judean Desert became home to a thriving monastic movement in the Holy Land. Hundreds of monks lived in the harsh, arid climate, sleeping in natural caves, studying, praying and working at monasteries. Several monastic communities are still active today.

The Monastery of St. Theodosius (Greek Orthodox) situated east of Bethlehem. It was instituted in the fifth century by St. Theodosius and holds his tomb. The monastery is still active today.

Mosaic floor in the ancient Martyrius Monastery

Mar Saba Monastery was one of the most important monastic centers in the Holy Land. It sits on the slope above the Kidron Valley. It holds the tomb of St. Sabas who founded it in the fifth century A.D. This Greek Orthodox monastery is still active; it is closed to women. Its exterior is one of the most impressive in the Holy Land.

The Ancient Martyrius Monastery is a large Byzantine monastery which was uncovered in a residential area at Ma'aleh Adumim east of Jerusalem on the road to Jericho. It was originally founded by the monk Martyrius in the fifth century A.D. Later, the monastery enlarged and became a central monastery in the Judean Desert.

The Dead Sea

The lowest point on the face of the earth is the Dead Sea. Its surface lies 400 meters (1290 feet) below sea level. Its high mineral content gave the sea its Hebrew name, "The Salt Sea." Accordingly, almost no vegetation or animal life occurs there, thus the name "Dead Sea."

Below: Dead Sea
Below Right: Wild ibex in the Oasis and Nature Reserve of Ein Gedi, west of the Dead Sea shore

The minerals found in and around the Dead Sea have proven useful for commercial, agricultural and industrial purposes. The Dead Sea is also well known as a tourist recreational area with its natural health facilities. Guests can relax on the beach, float on the surface of the water and bathe near the sea in thermo-mineral waters.

Another tourist resort in the area is the town of **Arad**, situated 24 km (15 miles) west of the Dead Sea between the Judean Desert and the Negev. Near the town, lies **Tel Arad**, the mound of ancient Arad, an important city in the Canaanite and Israelite periods.

Above the southern point of the Dead Sea **Mount Sodom** rises into the sky. Tradition holds this to be the area of the ill-fated cities Sodom and Gomorrah. According to Genesis God destroyed these cities for their grotesque corruption. When Lot's wife looked back at the city as fire and sulfur rained down upon it, she immediately turned into a pillar of salt (Gen. 19:24-26).

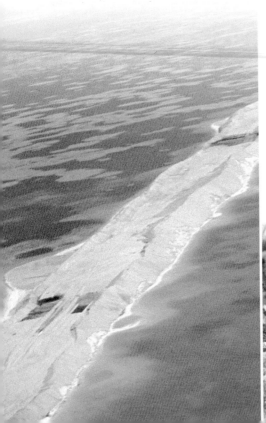

Qumran

Khirbet Qumran became famous in the 1940s and 50s when Bedouins and archaeologists discovered caves containing hundreds of scrolls from the Second Temple period. These scrolls became known as the **Dead Sea Scrolls**. The documents, written on papyrus, parchment and copper were hidden in jars and preserved for nearly two thousand years as a result of the area's arid climate. The scroll collection included books of the Hebrew Bible, commentaries on Scripture, and extra-biblical literature. Perhaps the most famous scroll is the Isaiah Scroll, which predated the earliest known copy of Isaiah by one thousand years. Some of the most interesting scrolls are sectarian writings relevant to the special beliefs and life-style of one sect's people.

Near the caves archaeologists discovered the ruins of a settlement called **Qumran** which is probably connected to the scrolls.

Many believe that the Essenes, a Jewish sect, occupied the site and was responsible for copying and composing the Dead Sea Scrolls. They thrived during the Second Temple period, the same time Jesus walked, taught and healed. Some say that just like John the Baptist, members of this group considered themselves called to the wilderness to prepare the way for God's visitation (Isa. 40:3).

Today tourists can view many of the Dead Sea Scrolls at the **Shrine of the Book** in Jerusalem.

Masada

Masada stands on a mountain in the Judean Desert overlooking the Dead Sea. According to the historian Flavius Josephus, the high priest Jonathan fortified the site and named it "Metzada," meaning "fortress." Some scholars consider this Jonathan to have been Alexander Jannaeus; others point to Jonathan Maccabaeus. Later Herod the Great, who became king of Judea under Roman appointment in 37 B.C., decided to make Masada a safe haven. He had fortifications and magnificent palaces built for himself and his entourage.

When the Jews revolted against Rome (A.D. 66), the Romans responded with massive power. Under Titus the Roman legions laid siege to Jerusalem, ultimately destroying the city and its temple in A.D. 70. A group of Jewish rebels known as "Zealots" (or, according to some scholars, "Sicarii") encamped in the safety of this fortress. Despite a total siege of the mountain, according to Josephus, almost one thousand Jews managed to hold off the enormous Roman force. They continued to hold the place for more than three years after the destruction of Jerusalem. However in A.D. 73, the Roman governor Flavius Silva marched against Masada with the Roman Tenth Legion. When it became clear that the Romans would prevail, the Zealots led by Eleazar ben Yair (Eleazar son of Jair), decided to commit mass suicide rather than fall into the hands of their hated enemy (Josephus, *Jewish Wars* 7.8.1ff.). When the Romans conquered Masada, they heard the story from two women who had concealed themselves in caverns. The Romans were astounded. "Nor could they do other than wonder at the courage of their resolution, and at the immovable contempt of death which so great a number of them had shown, when they went through with such an action as that was" (Josephus, *Jewish Wars* 7.9.2).

Today Masada is a favorite attraction for visitors to the Holy Land. They can see the great finds left by Herod and later by the Zealots. The finds recall the heroic defensive effort made by the Jews and the tragic fall of Masada.

Tel Aviv

Tel Aviv was founded in 1909 as the first modern Jewish city, north of Jaffa. Since then it has grown at a rapid pace. Today Tel Aviv, including Jaffa (Yafo) within its municipal boundaries, is a pulsating, vibrant, modern city. It offers residents and tourists alike a wide variety of activities. Situated on the Mediterranean coast in the center of modern Israel, Tel Aviv has become the country's financial and cultural center.

As a financial and administrative center, the city serves as the headquarters of many public and private companies. It is the administrative center for all the major banks, political parties, news organizations and foreign embassies.

As an educational, cultural and art center, Tel Aviv has several institutions of higher learning. The city has many museums and art galleries. Perhaps the best known is the Diaspora Museum.

Other museums in the city include the Tel Aviv Museum of Art and the Land of Israel Museum. As a center for performance and theater, the city offers a variety of theaters and show halls. The city is also the home of the Israel Philharmonic Orchestra and the New Israel Opera House.

Tel Aviv offers a wide variety of hospitality and entertainment, from deluxe hotels to a host of restaurants, cafes, pubs and nightclubs. There are open markets and shopping malls. To top it all off, the city possesses magnificent beaches on the Mediterranean with a lengthy stretch of white sand. Tourists can relax, swim, sun themselves and enjoy a variety of water sports.

Despite its rather hectic pace, it is possible to find many well-kept and quiet parks throughout Tel Aviv. The municipal slogan for Tel Aviv is "The City That Never Stops!"

Left: The "Carmel Market"   Below: An aerial view of Tel Aviv

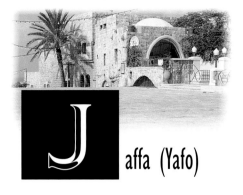

J affa (Yafo)

St. Peter's Church, Old Jaffa

Jaffa, in Hebrew "Yafo," ancient "Joppa," is one of the oldest cities in the Holy Land. Its beauty is engraved in the minds of all those who have visited it over the centuries.

It is first mentioned in Egyptian sources as one of the cities conquered by Thutmose III in the fifteenth century B.C. From ancient times it has served as a port city. Many pilgrims first encountered the Holy Land in Jaffa, the "gateway" to the rest of the land. In the Old Testament, King Huram of Tyre sent cedar timber to Solomon for building the temple through the port of Joppa (2 Chron. 2:2-16). It was also the harbor from which Jonah departed on his ill-fated journey to Tarshish (Jon 1:3).

In the New Testament Peter visited Joppa and resuscitated a woman who had died (Acts 9:36-42). Later, while staying with Simon the tanner in Joppa, Peter had a vision which led him to take the gospel to Cornelius, a Roman centurion in Caesarea (Acts 10:9-16).

According to one tradition, the **House of Simon the Tanner** lies in the Old City on the hill above the port. **The Old City** has been preserved in the same style as it was during the Ottoman period. The town contains narrow alleyways combined with modern art galleries and shops. Artifacts recovered from the site are on view in the square of Old Jaffa and in the **Museum of Antiquities of Tel Aviv-Jaffa**.

At the **Fisherman's Wharf**, open restaurants offer sea food and other middle-eastern delicacies.

One of the favorite attractions of Jaffa is its **Flea Market**. It is a place for tourists to "bargain" with some of the best deal-makers in the world.

The fisherman's wharf at Jaffa

The Southern Regions of the Holy Land

The southern regions of the Holy Land consist mainly of desert. They include the Negev and the Arava and stretch south to the Red Sea. This region contains broad expanses of beautiful scenery. The "primeval" landscape offers visitors spectacular views of desert country, oases and ancient cities next to new and modern towns.

In this region visitors discover the most outstanding geological phenomena in the Holy Land. The craters, streams and canyons, whose sides have been laid bare over the centuries in ever-deepening ravines, provide a unique window through which we can watch geological history unfold.

In spite of the desert conditions, people have inhabited this area for thousands of years. Indeed the Israelites passed through this region after the exodus from Egypt in the thirteenth century B.C. The Negev is mentioned many times in the Hebrew Bible, often translated simply as "south." It has special significance because of its position geographically between Asia and Africa. The international route joining the Red Sea and the Mediterranean passes through the Negev. Since ancient times the Negev and the Red Sea have served as major routes linking Asia and the Far East to Africa and the West.

With the creation of the modern State of Israel in 1948 this area has again begun to flourish. Modern settlements stand today as a proud reminder of Israel's promising future.

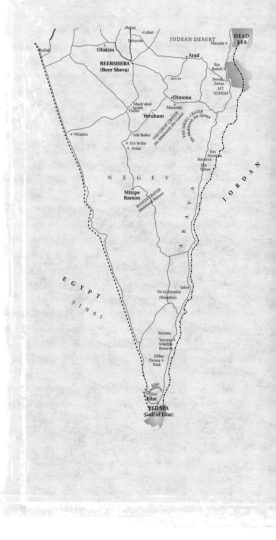

Negev

Arava

Beersheba (Beer Sheva)

After God commanded the patriarch Abraham to leave Haran, he traveled to the land of Canaan.

In the center of the city is **Abraham's Well**. Conflict erupted between Abraham and Abimelech, the king of Gerar, over the water rights to the well. Later, next to this well Abraham made a covenant with Abimelech, settling the issue by recognizing Abraham as the true owner of the well. So it was that, after Abraham, Isaac lived there and Beersheba became a symbol for the heritage of God's people.

They named this place Beer-sheba, from the Hebrew "Beer" meaning "well" and "Shevu'a" (oath) or "Shiv'a" (seven) (Gen. 21:31, 26:33).

Today Beersheba serves as the capital of the south. This administrative center also has a large industrial complex, a university with a center for desert studies, a hospital, a cultural arts center and shopping malls.

Above: Abraham's Well

The Bedouin in the Negev

Bedouin Market, Beersheba

The Bedouins are known for their nomadic ways and their intimate knowledge of the desert and its mystique. In earlier days they would move from place to place with all their worldly possessions in search of water and grass for their animals. In modern Israel, their lifestyle has changed and many have started moving into permanent settlements. Today there are a number of Bedouin settlements. Their largest center, **Rahat**, is only a few miles north of Beersheba.

Nabatean Towns in the Negev

The Nabateans, people of Arab origin, reached the Negev in the fourth century B.C. They travelled along the "Spice route," carrying herbs, spices, perfumes and treasures from northern Arabia and Transjordan to the Mediterranean. Their capital was Petra, a nearly impregnable city strategically located in Transjordan.

Along these routes they set up road stations, fortresses and trading centers. In the middle of the first century A.D., they lost their hold on the caravan trade and at the same time began to change their nomadic life to one of permanent settlements. These became important settlements during the Roman and Byzantine eras and their impressive remnants can still be seen today. During the Byzantine period, the Nabateans began to accept Christianity and due to this we can find churches beside dwelling quarters, workshops and cemeteries. In these sites one discovers some of the "secrets" of Nabatean life which helped to provide water to the inhabitants all year round.

Above:The Nabtean city of Avdat

Modern Settlements

Interest in the Negev was rekindled by Jewish settlements in the region prior to the formation of the State of Israel.. Pioneers arrived aiming to reclaim and settle the Negev. One of the main activists for this policy was David Ben Gurion, the first Prime Minister of the State of Israel. He had planned a great future for the Negev, recognizing the strategic importance and economic potential of the region. Yet the undertaking was not easy. During the War of Independence (1948), many hard battles were fought in the area and the Jewish settlements were cut off from the rest of the country for some time. With the establishment of the state, resettling the Negev became a priority. The Negev once again began to thrive. One of the best known settlements is **Kibbutz Sde Boker**, where Ben Gurion and his wife Paula made their home. Today his original cabin is a museum that contains his library and study, his important papers and many gifts he received from heads of state and people from all over the world.

Ben Gurion Memorial National Park

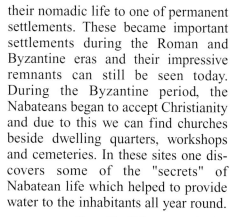

L ife in the Desert

As one travels south, it is obvious that fresh water sources become more and more scarce. Despite this the desert is not desolate. Springs, oases and pastures dot the desert landscape.

Plants and animals have found ways to adapt to this harsh environment. Yet even these live primarily near the oases and springs.

Ein Avdat (the Spring of Avdat) is camouflaged springs in the middle of the desert. The springs and their surroundings are like small desert oases, teeming with vigorous plant life. The site is under the jurisdiction of the National Park Authority.

The Yotvata Wildlife Reserve (Hai Bar Yotvata) provides visitors an opportunity to view the Negev's wildlife. Located north of Eilat next to Kibbutz Yotvata, this open nature reserve contains several interesting exhibits.

The Negev Craters are comprised of three craters formed as a result of soil and rock erosion. Initially, the elements opened giant holes in the soft face of the earth. As the erosion continued, deeper, more ancient geological layers were exposed, revealing the fascinating multi-colored geological history of the earth.

The largest of the three craters in the Negev is the **Ramon Crater**, southeast of Mitzpe Ramon. It contains a unique nature reserve with an open geological park consisting of sandstone formations and fossils. In addition, visitors encounter the remains of several ancient civilizations and unique plant and animal life.

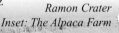

Ramon Crater
Inset: The Alpaca Farm

Eilat

Above: The Dolphin Reef
Below: "Mushroom" sandstone, Timna Park

The beautiful city of Eilat is situated at the intersection of the desert and the sea, at the foot of picturesque mountains. Today, it serves as both a port and vacation destination on the Red Sea (Gulf of Eilat).

In the Old Testament the town is referred to as Elath (or Eloth) and is mentioned in conjunction with Ezion - geber. On their way into the Prom-ised Land the Israelites passed by these two points. (Deuterononmy 2:8). King Solomon built a fleet of ships on the northern shore of the Red Sea and used it for trade with Ophir (1 Kings 9:26). Today, in addition to being a port city, Eilat also serves as a land bridge between Israel and Egypt to the south, and Israel and Jordan to the east.

The moderate climate and comfortable tourist atmosphere have earned Eilat an excellent reputation. The contrast between the sea and the mountains creates an awe-inspiring yet pastoral vista. Add to this the magnificent, secluded beaches, luxury hotels, restaurants and pubs along the shore, aquatic facilities, cruise ships and other entertainment, Eilat has all the ingredients to guarantee its guests a memorable holiday.

Eilat's Coral Beach Reserve may be one of the best known coral habitats in the world. The Underwater Observatory and Aquarium provide tourists the opportunity to see this "magical underwater world."

Timna Park

Located on the Arava, north of Eilat, Timna Park is situated in the Timna Valley. Guests to the park experience a magical world of natural geological formations and incredible vistas. The imprint of human culture alongside nature makes Timna Park one of the most impressive sites in the Holy Land.

The site in the park includes:

 The "Mushroom" and "Solomon's Pillars" are both giant formations of red sandstone carved by natural erosion.

Ancient copper mines demonstrate that mining began here in the Chalcolithic period around 4000 B.C. and lasted until the Roman period.

Egyptian figures depicted in stone wall carvings. Ruins of an Egyptian temple. Timna Lake, an artificial lake created from subterranean waters.

CHRONOLOGICAL TABLE OF HOLY LAND HISTORY

PERIOD (B.C.)			SUB-DIVISION		MAJOR EVENTS
8000	Neolithic		Pre-Pottery		First permanent villages
		5500	Pottery		Invention of pottery
4500	Chalcolithic				Temple at Ein Gedi
3300	Bronze Age	3300	Early Bronze Age		First cities
	(Canaanite Period)	2200	Middle Bronze Age		Patriarchal Period Abraham arrives in Canaan
				18th 14th	Beginning of Egyptian rule El Amarna letters
		1550	Late Bronze Age	13th	Israelite Exodus from Egypt led by Moses
1200	Iron Age (Israelite Period)			13-12th	Conquest of Canaan by the Israelites under Joshua Settlement of the tribes
				12-11th 12th	Judges Period Invasion of "Sea People" Philistine expansion
		1020	United Monarchy	c.1020 1004	Reign of King Saul King David David conquers Jerusalem
			Beginning of First Temple Period	965	Solomon reigns Solomon builds the First Temple
		c.930	Divided Monarchy		Regions of Judah (south) and Israel (north)
				722	Invasion of Assyria
587/6	Babylonian Period			586	Destruction of Jerusalem and the First Temple by Babylon Babylonian Exile
539/8	Persian Period		Return to Zion Beginning of Second Temple Period	515 457;445	Cyrus decrees return of Jews The Second Temple Dedicated Ezra and Nehemiah
333/2	Hellenistic Period				Conquest by Alexander the Great
		301	Rule of Ptolemies (Egypt)		
		198	Rule of Seleucids (Syria)	167	Maccabean (Hasmonean) Revolt
		141	Hasmonean Dynasty Rule	164	Rededication of the Temple Jewish independent state
63	Roman Period				Pompey conquers Jerusalem
		37-4	Reign of Herod the Great		Herod Rebuilds the Temple Mount
				c.6/4	Birth of Jesus

PERIOD (A.D.)		SUB-DIVISION		MAJOR EVENTS
Roman Period (continued) Important writings New Testament Josephus Flavius: The Jewish War; Antiquities Mishna (Jewish Oral Law)	6	Roman Procurators (26 Pontius Pilate) Jerusalem as Roman colony	c.30/33 66 70 73 132-135	Jesus' ministry Crucifixion and Resurrection of Jesus Ministry of Apostles Jewish Revolt against Rome Destruction of the Second Temple Roman siege of Masada Bar Kokhba Revolt Jerusalem - Aelia Capitolina
324 Important writings Babylonian Talmud Jerusalem/Palestinian Talmud		**Byzantine Period**	527 614 628	Constantine recognizes Christianity Building of Major Churches Reign of Emperor Justinian I Persian invasion Christians Rule - Heraclius
638		**Early Arab-Muslim Period**		Umayyad Caliphs Abassid Rule Seljuk Rule
638		Umayyad Caliphs Abassid Rule Seljuk Rule	691-2	Jerusalem conquered by Arabs Building of Dome of the Rock El-Aqsa Mosque
1099	1099	**Crusader Period** — First Crusade Crusade and Ayyubid Rules	1187	Jerusalem under Christians Horns of Hattin Battle Failure of the Crusades Acco-the Crusaders' Capital (Mongol invasions)
1291		**Late Arab Period** — Fatimid and Mameluke	1291	End of Crusader Kingdom
1516/17		**Ottoman Period** — Suleiman the Magnificent	1799 1831/2 1882 1909	Building of Jerusalem present walls Napoleon attacks Muhammad Ali of Egypt First New Jewish settlements Zionist Organization Tel Aviv; Kibbutz Deganiah
1516/17	1914	First World War	1917	Balfour Declaration promises the Jews a National Home
1917/18 Holocaust in Europe	1922 1939	**British** Mandate Second World War	1947	Arab Riots against Jews New Jewish settlements UN votes for Jewish State
1948 ff		**State of Israel**	1949 1956 1967 1969 1973 1978 1982 1993 1994	Israeli War of Independence Jerusalem divided between Israel and Jordan Jurisdiction Mass Jewish immigration Sinai (Suez) Campaign Six Day War. Jerusalem comes under control of Israel War of Attrition with Egypt Yom Kippur War Peace agreement with Egypt War in Lebanon Declaration of Principles of Peace signed by Israel and Palestinian Authorities Peace Treaty with Jordan

INDEX OF PLACE NAMES